AIRFLOW

Martin Simons

AE Press
Melbourne
1984

Australasian Educa Press Pty. Ltd.
74 Railway Road (PO Box 186)
Blackburn, Vic. 3130

Telephone: (03) 878 0466

First published in 1984 by AE Press
© 1984, Martin Simons

National Library of Australia
Cataloguing-in-Publication entry
Simons, Martin, 1930-
  Airflow.
  Includes index.
  ISBN 0 86787 024 9.
  ISBN 0 86787 045 1 (pbk.).
  1. Air flow. I. Title.
533'.62

Cover design and layout by John van Loon
Illustrations by John Schout
Typeset by Town & Country Typesetters, Abbotsford, Victoria
Printed by Dominion Press Hedges & Bell, Victoria,
Australia

Contents

the force of the wind

Because the air is invisible, people at one time thought it was some kind of spirit, or that the winds were mysterious forces controlled by various gods, sometimes helpful, sometimes mischievous and often extremely dangerous. It was many centuries before it was realised that air is a material substance and that its behaviour can be explained physically. Even now, engineers and architects are sometimes surprised by the effects of wind, and a good deal remains to be discovered. Some examples of damage done by the air are shown in photographs 1 and 2. In gales, minor damage may affect houses,

1 The roof of this small house at a coastal site has been lifted off. Where the walls have fallen, they have gone outwards rather than inwards. This is explained in the text. (Adelaide *Advertiser*)

2 The Tacoma Narrows bridge during the wind storm in 1940. The gale caused the bridge to twist to and fro until it collapsed. The photograph was taken from a cine film made at the time.

tall buildings, aerials and towers. A severe gale does more harm, and whirlwind storms, known as *tornadoes*, can bring total destruction to a local district. Tropical *cyclones*, typhoons and hurricanes, which are very large whirlwinds, are capable of devastating extensive areas.

When the first scientific studies were done on wind damage, one of the early discoveries, very surprising to most people, was that when a house loses its roof in a high wind, it is usually lifted off the walls, not blown down. The whole roof may be raised and carried some distance before it falls. Even more puzzling, often a tall, steeply pitched roof still stands after the storm while lower buildings all around, with shallow, gently pitched roofs, are left open to the sky. If the entire roof of a building is not altogether removed, it is often found that a few tiles, or some of the steel roofing sheets, have been lifted off. These are frequently taken, not only from the part of the roof facing into the wind, but from the lee, or sheltered side. They seem to have been sucked off, rather than pushed down. If the walls do collapse, it is not the ones facing directly into the gale that go first, as a rule. The end walls of the house tend to fall outwards, sucked out rather than blown in, and it is only after they have gone that the front wall may be pushed over (Photo 1).

Streamlined and separated flow

Some of the reasons for these unexpected effects became clearer when it was discovered that there are two main kinds of air flow. Sometimes the air flows smoothly along, passing over and around things in its way. This is rather like the way water will pass along in a smooth channel and is called *streamlined flow*. If a small particle of air is imagined as tracing a line as it goes, the line in streamlined flow will be gently curved. The other main kind of flow is called *separated flow*. This is more like the roughness and turbulence seen in rivers at the foot of waterfalls, and the lines traced by the particles are very irregular.

A low-pitched roof does not make a very big obstacle to the wind, and the flow over it tends to be streamlined (Figure 3). There may be some separated flow under the eaves of the roof, but the pattern of the streamlines is generally smooth.

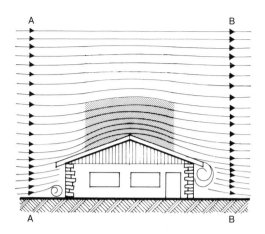

The same mass of air flows past B-B in each second as passes A-A. Hence flow over the house speeds up.

░ high speed flow region

3. Streamlined flow over a low-pitched roof.

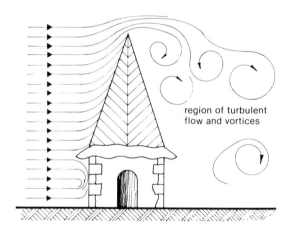

region of turbulent flow and vortices

4. Separated flow over a steeply pitched roof.

A steeply pitched roof may have stream-lined flow up the side facing the wind, but on the lee the flow breaks away or separates and behind the roof there is a lot of turbulence (Figure 4). Often there are rotating swirls, called *vortices* in the separated flow.

When the wind flows smoothly over a house, the streamlines have to curve and the speed of flow increases. Air is not like snow or sand; it cannot pile up in heaps around an obstruction, but flows like a fluid. The same mass of air must flow away from the obstruction as flows towards it, in each time interval. Since the streamlines are curved to get round the obstacle, the distance to be covered is greater so to keep up with the rest of the moving air, the flow must accelerate.

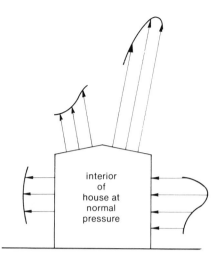

interior of house at normal pressure

The length and direction of each arrow indicates the pressure forces measured at each point. There are forces on the wall facing the wind tending to push it over, but the lifting forces on the roof are much greater.

5. Wind pressure measurements on an actual house with a low-pitched roof.

To make any mass accelerate, a force is needed, and the energy required for this force must be supplied from the air. Energy of movement is called *kinetic energy*, and this must be increased. The *potential energy* of the air has to be reduced to supply more kinetic energy. This reduction in potential energy shows up as a reduction of the air pressure as the flow speeds up. The more the flow speeds up, the lower the air pressure. On a low pitched roof, the smoothly curved flow causes a reduction of pressure over the whole area, especially where the flow speed is greatest (Figure 5). Inside the house, the air pressure is usually close to the normal pressure, depending on its height above sea level and the weather pattern. The difference in pressures between the inside and outside may be enough to lift the roof off.

Around the ends of the house the same kind of thing may happen. The streamlines curve around, the flow speeds up and the pressure falls outside the end walls. The difference between the inside and outside pressure tends to force the walls outwards. Figure 6 shows the pattern of airflow measured round some full-sized buildings. A simple direction indicator like that shown in Figure 7 may be used to construct such diagrams.

With a steeply pitched roof, although the turbulent flow may be rough, it is on average slower. This is why people can find shelter from strong winds behind buildings or walls.

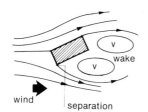

Plan of a single building

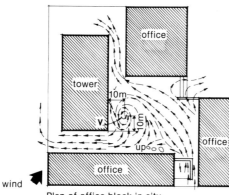

Plan of office block in city
Note the vortices

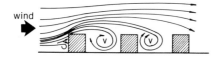

End view of three school buildings

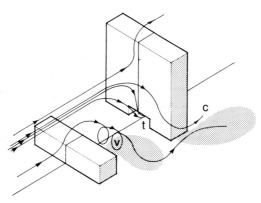

v - vortex-flow
t - through-flow
c - corner-stream

6. Flow of air round buildings in a wind;
note the *vortices* 'v'.

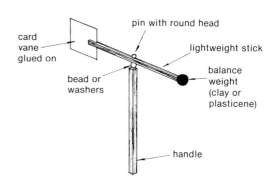

7. A simple wind direction indicator which may be
used for investigating flow around buildings.

In open country, 'wind breaks' of trees are
often planted to shelter isolated homesteads
or prevent damage to delicate crops. On the
lee side of a tall building, because the flow is
slowed down instead of speeded up, the
pressure may rise almost to the normal value.
Kinetic energy is converted to potential
energy. There may still be damage here and
there, owing to the vortices, but the whole
roof is less likely to lift.

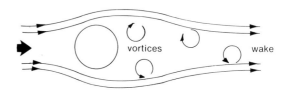

8. Flow around a tall chimney or circular tower. Note
how the flow begins to divide before reaching the
tower, and the separated flow behind the obstruction.

When the wind strikes a tall tower or a
chimney, it tends to flow round it rather than
over the top. This almost always causes flow
separation on the lee side. There is a 'wake'
behind the tower, which trails off downwind
for a large distance, somewhat like the wake
of a boat moving through water. This wake
will be very turbulent. There will usually be
many powerful vortices tending to twist the
flow from side to side (Figure 8). If there is
another tower, or a series of chimneys, which
is struck by the wake, the result may be
damaging to them even while the first one
remains unharmed.

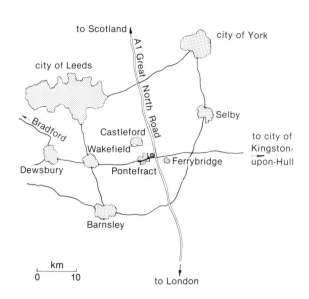

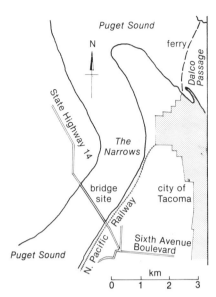

9. Sketch map showing location of Ferrybridge in England.

10. Sketch map to show position of the old Tacoma Narrows Bridge, Washington State, USA.

11 Research into the effects of winds is often done in wind tunnels. This one is at the James Cook University at Townsville, in Queensland. Air is drawn through the tunnel by a large fan driven by a powerful electric motor. (James Cook University)

Sometimes both kinds of damage may occur. A very serious example which occurred in 1965 in England, was when a whole group of large cooling towers at Ferrybridge Power Station collapsed in a gale (Figure 9). They had been standing for years, apparently safely, until this disaster. The cause was found to be the combined effects of streamlined suction on the curved sides of the towers, and wake turbulence.

Bridges are also sometimes damaged or destroyed by wind. A notorious example was in 1879 when the Tay Bridge in Scotland was blown down while carrying a full train load of passengers. The engineer who designed the bridge admitted that he had not made any special allowance for the force of the wind when doing the calculations. In more recent times, while wind pressure and pressure changes are always allowed for, some bridges have still proved unsafe in windy conditions. One that failed altogether was at Tacoma Narrows, USA, in 1940 (Figure 10 and Photo 2). This was a suspension bridge, a type in which the roadway hangs from strong steel cables. In a severe gale, the bridge began to lift up and twist to and fro. Soon it was almost *fluttering*, even though the roadway was supported by very strong girders, and finally it collapsed.

Before this bridge was replaced, many tests were made in a wind tunnel (Photo 11), on a scale model, to make the structure safer.

When the wind blows over hills, the streamlines behave in very much the same way as when the flow is obstructed by buildings. This is one of the reasons why the wind speed at the crest of a ridge is greater than over flat ground. This often has an effect on vegetation. Trees and other plants sensitive to strong winds will be unable to survive where flow speeds are higher. It is also quite common for the flow to separate behind a steep lee slope. There may be a region of 'dead' or nearly calm air on one side of the hill, with a fierce gale on the other (Figure 12).

The wind is also responsible for a great deal of soil erosion. Just as the flow of water in rivers or floods picks up and carries away pieces of rock and sand, the wind will move dust and sandy grains wherever these are exposed and loose enough to be carried off. Dust storms form, but the result most serious to farms, is the loss of topsoil and the damage to crops that may have been growing. Plant roots are exposed and die. This tends to leave the soil even more exposed, ready to be removed by the next strong wind.

Things to do:

1   Make a simple wind direction indicator similar to that shown in Figure 7, and, on a windy day, investigate the directions of wind flow around buildings. Locate any areas of 'dead' air and vortex flow and note the places where the wind speed seems unusually high. Use a simple *anemometer* (Figure 13) to measure wind speeds in various locations. Compare these with the wind speeds measured by the local Bureau of Meteorology. Try to explain any differences.

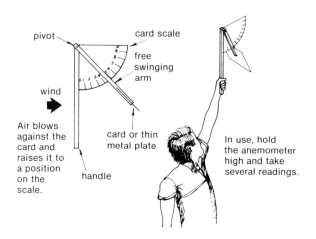

13. A simple anemometer which may be used for comparative flow speed measurements. For more accurate work, the anemometer should be calibrated against a standard instrument.

2   Make a *manometer* (Figure 14), and measure pressure changes around buildings in a strong wind.

3   Test different shapes of buildings in a simple wind tunnel with wool tufts to indicate flow directions. (A design for a wind tunnel is given in Figure 47.)

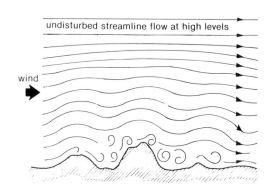

12. Wind flow over hills.

Things to find out:

1 Learn the Beaufort scale of winds and practise using it.

2 What is the strongest wind gust ever recorded in your district? What damage (if any) was done? Where does the local Bureau of Meteorology measure wind speeds and directions? What precautions are taken to get a fair result? What system is used in your region to warn people of expected high winds?

3 How do farmers try to avoid the effects of wind erosion on their soil?

Bernoulli's theorem

Daniel Bernoulli was one of several in his family who became famous. His particular interests were in science and engineering, especially the flow of fluids. He discovered the relationship between the speed of flow and pressure in a closed pipe. Most people already knew that if water, or any other fluid, was flowing through a pipe which varied in size, the flow was faster where the diameter of the pipe was smaller. Hose pipes or water taps can be made to squirt the fluid at very high speed by squeezing or closing part of the exit, for example. Bernoulli realised that the energy to make the fluid go faster must come from the pressure in the flow; the pressure on the sides must fall in the narrow part of the pipe. This is quite the opposite of what most people expect, but the fall of pressure can be measured (Figure 14).

Bernoulli's Theorem states that the pressure energy in a streamlined flow plus the kinetic energy of the fluid is constant. Where

p stands for pressure, V for the velocity and the Greek letter ϱ (rho) for the mass density of the fluid:

$$p + \frac{\varrho}{2} V^2 = \text{constant}$$

This means that if velocity increases, pressure must decrease, so long as the air density ϱ remains unchanged. One of the most important aspects of this discovery was the *square law* relating the effects of the flow to the speed. In Bernoulli's equation, the velocity is multiplied by itself, or squared. His work was concerned with incompressible liquids, but the equation proves to be very accurate for flow in all kinds of gases providing the speed is not too great. When the velocity approaches the speed of sound, the equation has to be modified to allow for the compressibility of gases. In such conditions, density also changes.

Since Bernoulli published his results in 1738, use has been made of the theorem in many ways, with air and gases as well as liquids. For example, in the very simple sort of spray gun used by artists, and sometimes for scent sprays, a flow of air, forced through a nozzle by someone blowing or squeezing a small rubber bulb, causes a drop in pressure at the narrowest part of the nozzle. Just at this place, the end of a second tube is placed so the reduced pressure sucks the paint or scent from a container below. Some of the more elaborate spray guns used in factories work in the same way, although the air is blown through the nozzle by a pump.

After Bernoulli, it was nearly a hundred years before anyone realised that the same principles could be used to enable humans to fly.

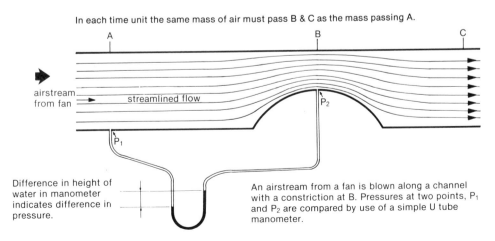

In each time unit the same mass of air must pass B & C as the mass passing A.

airstream from fan

streamlined flow

Difference in height of water in manometer indicates difference in pressure.

An airstream from a fan is blown along a channel with a constriction at B. Pressures at two points, P_1 and P_2 are compared by use of a simple U tube manometer.

14. Demonstration of Bernoulli's theorem.

Beaufort Scale of Wind Speed

Beaufort No.	Seaman's description of wind	Terms used in Weather Bureau forecasts	Wind speed		Description of sea	On land
			in knots	in m./sec.		
0	Calm	Calm	Less than 1	Less than 0.3	Sea like a mirror	Smoke rises vertically
1	Light air	Light	1-3	0.3-1.5	Ripples, no foam crests	Smoke drifts
2	Light breeze	Light	4-6	1.6-3.3	Small wavelets, crests have a glassy appearance and do not break	Leaves on trees move slightly
3	Gentle breeze	Gentle	7-10	3.4-5.4	Large wavelets, crests begin to break. Perhaps scattered white caps	Flags flap, leaves and twigs on trees moving
4	Moderate breeze	Moderate	11-16	5.5-8.0	Small waves becoming longer. Fairly frequent white caps	Dust raised, branches of trees swaying
5	Fresh breeze	Fresh	17-21	8.1-10.7	Moderate waves, taking a more pronounced long form. Many white caps, some spray	Small trees swaying
6	Strong breeze	Strong	22-27	10.8-13.8	Large waves begin to form. Extensive white caps everywhere, some spray	Large branches swaying
7	Moderate gale (high wind)	Strong	28-33	13.9-17.1	Sea heaps up and white foam from breaking waves begins to be blown in well-marked streaks along the direction of the wind	Large trees swaying, walking against wind is difficult
8	Fresh gale	Gale	34-40	17.2-20.7	Moderately high waves of greater length. Edges of crests break into spindrift. The foam is blown in well-marked streaks along the direction of wind	Twigs and small branches breaking, leaves stripping, dust storms
9	Strong gale	Gale	41-47	20.8-24.4	High waves. Dense streaks of foam along the direction of the wind. Spray may affect visibility. Sea begins to roll	Large branches breaking, roof damage likely, hard to stand
10	Whole gale (heavy gale)	Whole gale	48-55	24.5-28.3	Very high waves with long overhanging crests. The surface of the sea takes on a white appearance. The rolling of the sea becomes heavy and shocklike. Visibility is affected	Whole trees uprooted, some damage to many buildings
11	Storm	Whole gale	56-65	28.4-33.5	Exceptionally high waves. The sea is completely covered with long white patches of foam. Visibility is affected. Small- and medium-sized ships are lost to view for long periods	Widespread damage to buildings and vegetation
12	Hurricane, Typhoon, Cyclone	Hurricane Cyclone	Above 65	Above 33.6	The air is filled with foam and spray. Sea completely white with driving spray. Visibility very seriously affected	Widespread disaster, houses destroyed, forests uprooted, etc.

chapter 2

the atmosphere

The air which forms the Earth's *atmosphere* is a mixture of gases, chiefly nitrogen (approximately 78 per cent) and oxygen (approximately 21 per cent). All the other gases, such as argon, carbon dioxide, helium etc, total less than 1 per cent of dry air (Figure 15). The atmosphere at lower levels is never totally dry. Water vapour is present in varying proportions and is not included in the percentages given above. Like the other gases in the air, water vapour is quite invisible to human eyes. Clouds, mist and fog are actually liquid water in very fine droplets or sometimes tiny ice particles, suspended in the air. A cloud forms when the water vapour condenses and so becomes visible. If the droplets become too large to be held aloft in suspension, they fall as rain. A cloud may disappear soon after it has formed. The water droplets evaporate and return to invisible vapour. The formation and evaporation of clouds may be observed easily on many occasions by watching a single *cumulus cloud* for twenty or thirty minutes. Time-lapse photography can often show these changes in a very exciting fashion (Photo 16).

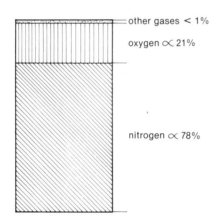

15. The composition of dry air.

The motion of clouds gives some idea of how the air moves although most of the time the flow is invisible and has to be imagined.

Dust and smoke may also be watched carefully to see how the air containing them is moving. The very high, feathery *cirrus clouds* often visible in fine weather, are formed from innumerable very small ice crystals and the streaky appearance of the sky on these occasions may indicate the flow direction at very high altitudes, usually different from the winds lower down.

16   A time lapse sequence of photographs showing the development and decay of a single small cumulus cloud. The camera was set up on a tripod pointing directly downwind. In the first photograph the cloud is still growing but as it drifts away with the wind it begins to evaporate. A few minutes later it had gone entirely. The photographs were taken at intervals of one minute. (Author)

The atmosphere is often said to be like an ocean, at the bottom of which people, animals and plants live. Flying creatures such as birds and insects may then be compared to fish and shellfish in the sea. These ideas are quite useful because the air, although gaseous, does behave in many ways like a liquid. We are used to the idea that liquids have mass and exert pressures, and that they flow. It is easier to see currents in fluids but air currents and flows are just as real. Fish and other swimming animals are shaped to enable them to move easily through the water. It has been found that similar shapes are required for easy movement through air (Figure 17).

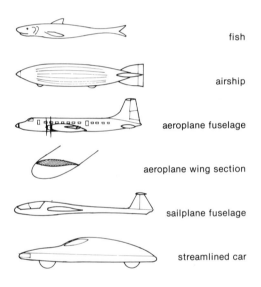

17. Bodies shaped for easy movement through fluids.

Solid particles in water are sometimes held in suspension, just as dust, ice and water droplets may be in the air. It is sometimes possible to imitate an invisible air flow by using water instead of air. The pattern of flow is often very similar.

The idea of the atmosphere as an ocean of air should not be taken too far. There are some important differences. Air is compressible. Liquids such as water are hardly compressible at all, and under normal conditions of temperature and pressure, they are regarded as quite incompressible. For instance, the hydraulic brake system of most ordinary automobiles depends on the practically incompressible nature of the brake fluid.

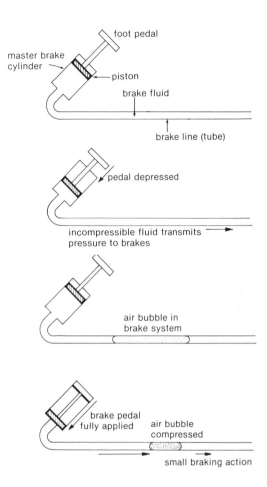

18. How a bubble of air may affect a car braking system.

If a bubble of air gets into the brake lines, a very dangerous situation arises (Figure 18). When the driver presses the brake pedal, instead of applying force directly via the fluid to the brakes, much of the energy goes into compressing the air that has leaked into the system and the brakes lose most of their effect. This is why cars should have their brakes 'bled' after re-filling with brake fluid, or after repair work has been done.

Anyone who has pumped up a car or bicycle tyre knows that a large amount of air can be forced into a confined space. If 'over-inflated', the tyre may burst, but if the container is rigid and strong enough, large masses of air may be compressed into small volumes. As the pressure rises, the density of the gas becomes greater. This cannot normally be done with liquids. Scuba and deep sea divers know that as they go deeper the pressure of the fluid on their bodies increases rapidly, in proportion to the weight of the water above their level. The *density*

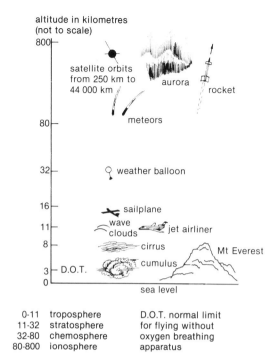

altitude in kilometres
(not to scale)

800 — satellite orbits
from 250 km to
44 000 km   aurora   rocket

meteors

80 —

32 —   ♀ weather balloon

16 —   ✈ sailplane
11 —   wave clouds   jet airliner
8 —   cirrus   Mt Everest
3 —   D.O.T.   cumulus
0 —
sea level

0-11	troposphere	D.O.T. normal limit
11-32	stratosphere	for flying without
32-80	chemosphere	oxygen breathing
80-800	ionosphere	apparatus

19. The atmosphere.

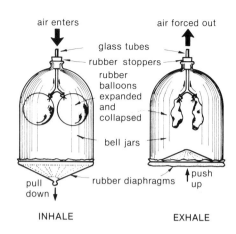

air enters   air forced out

glass tubes
rubber stoppers
rubber balloons expanded and collapsed
bell jars
rubber diaphragms
pull down   push up

INHALE   EXHALE

An apparatus that shows how breathing occurs

20. How humans breathe. Note that the lung is not like a rubber balloon in structure. Its internal appearance resembles a sponge.

remains the same. In the atmosphere, the pressure at depth is more than it is at higher levels, but because of the compressibility of the gas mixture, the density low down is also much greater. In a deep mine, the air pressure and density are both more than at the ground surface, and above ground both decrease as the *altitude* increases. One important result is that the atmosphere has nothing comparable to the surface of the sea. The atmospheric density decreases gradually to the nearly perfect emptiness or vacuum of space. At sea level, the density of the air, under natural conditions, is about 1.22 kg/cubic metre; that is, 1.22 kg mass of air occupies a cubic metre of space. Changes of air pressure associated with the changing weather pattern, change the density too. At altitudes about 5500 metres above sea level, corresponding to some mountain peaks, the density is about half the sea level average. At 10 000 metres, a height often reached by jet airliners, the density is about one third of that at sea level. At greater altitudes, pressure and density continue to fall; some air is still present at levels of several hundred kilometres.

Balloons and airships, which are commonly termed 'lighter-than-air' vessels, are not like seagoing boats and ships because they cannot float on any surface. They remain wholly within the atmosphere. Aeroplanes and helicopters, which are termed 'heavier-than-air' craft, cannot fly to the top of the atmosphere because they depend on the flow of air over wings and rotors to support them (Figure 19). Although rocket motors can accelerate a vehicle, such as a satellite or space craft, out of the atmosphere entirely, the motors used in ordinary aircraft — jet and piston engines — require atmospheric air and are incapable of operation if the air density and pressure fall too low.

Breathing at high altitudes

The reduction of air density is the main reason why breathing becomes more difficult for humans and animals at high altitudes. When we breath in, the muscles of the diaphragm and chest expand the lung cavities and the external pressure normally ensures that these cavities are filled with air which enters through the nose and mouth (Figure 20).

About one fifth of the mass entering is oxygen, needed by the blood to keep us alive. At an altitude of 5500 metres, the lung space is the same but only about half the total mass of air will enter. It will be under lower pressure too, making it more difficult for the blood to absorb it. Although there is still 21 per cent oxygen in the mixture, the body has available to it only half the usual quantity. If

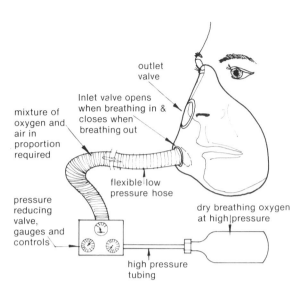

22 A glider pilot preparing for a high altitude soaring flight, wearing his oxygen breathing apparatus. (Theo Heimgartner)

21. Schematic diagram of a simple oxygen breathing system as used in aircraft.

we go much higher, even if the lungs are expanded as much as possible, the air density and pressure are too low to support life. (Healthy people with good lung capacity can survive at somewhat greater heights than the unfit.)

There are two ways of enabling people to breathe at such heights. The simplest, used quite often by sailplane pilots, and sometimes by parachutists, is to take some pure, dry, oxygen to add to the breathed air (Figure 21 and Photo 22). A face mask is worn, and, depending on the height, a regulated quantity of oxygen is fed into the mask from a storage bottle so that what enters the lungs is an enriched mixture containing much more than 21 per cent of oxygen. Even at the reduced pressure, the blood receives an adequate supply up to about 10 000 metres. Above this level 100 percent oxygen is barely enough for most people. The pressure is too low to enable the blood to absorb the gas, even if the lungs are entirely full of oxygen. The reduced pressure can also cause the gases dissolved in the bloodstream, such as nitrogen, to form bubbles. The result is a very painful condition similar to the deep sea diver's 'bends' and possibly fatal.

The more common method for airliners and military aircraft is to use a pressure suit or pressure cabin (Figure 23). The passengers and crew are enclosed in a sealed space, and a pump forces air in from outside.

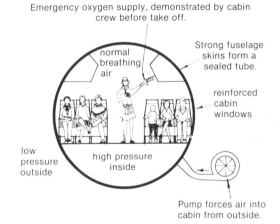

23. How a pressure cabin works.

The incoming air is very cold and at very low pressure. It is compressed and blown into the cabin or suit. Compression of any gas causes it to warm up, helping the internal temperature to be kept at a comfortable level. The pressure and density are maintained at a level roughly equivalent to about 1500 metres. Under these conditions normal breathing is possible. If the pressure cabin of an airliner develops a bad leak, pure oxygen is supplied to the passengers until the pilot can bring the aircraft to a lower level. Fortunately such emergencies are very rare, because if plunged suddenly from nearly normal air density to that prevailing at 10 000 metres, human beings usually collapse and lose consciousness within a few seconds.

Atmospheric layers

The atmosphere has been found to be arranged in fairly distinct layers, although the junctions between them are quite diffuse. The lowest layer, called the *troposphere*, is that which contains most of the water vapour, and in which the weather occurs. The temperature of the air at and near ground level changes a good deal from hour to hour. Because of cooling of the land during the night, the air at dawn is often warmer a few hundred metres up than it is immediately above the cold ground in the morning. Such early *temperature inversions* are nearly always present. As the land warms up after sunrise, the situation is normally reversed. The air is heated from below, by heat radiated from the surface of the Earth, rather than from above by the direct rays of the sun. On average the air cools with altitude until at around 11 000m it reaches approximately − 57.3 degrees Celsius. This level marks, roughly, the upper level of the troposphere. Higher up is the *stratosphere* where the temperature remains nearly constant at − 57.3°C up to about 30 km above ground, the start of the so-called chemosphere and higher still, the ionosphere. Ordinary aircraft never reach such levels although a few special research balloons have done so. Rockets and space vehicles can pass through the various layers into the near-vacuum of outer space.

The standard atmosphere

The atmosphere is always moving. The changes of pressure, temperature and humidity at ground levels are measured and published every day along with weather forecasts. In aeronautics, methods have been worked out which enable aircraft to be flown safely under widely varying conditions. An average, or *Standard Atmosphere* has been adopted internationally.

When designing new types or comparing different aircraft for performance (speed, cargo capacity, etc), engineers calculate everything as if the flights were all made in the International Standard Atmosphere. When flying, the pilot must also set the instruments, especially the altimeter, which indicates height, according to the International Standard Atmosphere.

Speed of sound m/s	Density kg/m³	km		Thousands of feet	Temp °C	Press. mb
299	0.040	25		80	− 52	28
298	0.047	24		75	− 54	35
298	0.055	23		70	− 55	45
297	0.065	22		65	− 56	57
296	0.076	21		60	− 56	72
295	0.089	20		55	− 56	92
295	0.104	19		50	− 56	117
295	0.122	18		45	− 56	148
295	0.142	17		40	− 56	188
295	0.166	16		35	− 54	239
295	0.195	15		30	− 44	301
295	0.228	14		25	− 34	377
295	0.267	13		20	− 25	466
295	0.312	12		15	− 15	572
295	0.365	11		10	− 5	697
299	0.414	10		5	− 5	843
304	0.467	9		Sea level	15	1013
308	0.526	8				
313	0.590	7				
317	0.660	6				
321	0.736	5				
325	0.819	4				
329	0.909	3				
333	1.007	2				
337	1.112	1				
340	1.225	Sea level				

Note: The uppermost level of 25 km represents the limit of this artificial atmosphere, but the real atmosphere continues far beyond, as shown in Figure 19.

24. The International Standard Atmosphere.

The altimeter works by measuring the air pressure (Figure 25). The dial of the instrument shows a fall in pressure as a gain of altitude. Before take-off, the pilot, if intending only to fly locally and for a short time, may set it to read zero at ground level. If it is planned to land at some other aerodrome, the instrument will be set to read in heights above sea level, since different airports are rarely at the same altitude. In either case, as the weather changes, the air pressure varies, so after some time the altimeter will be incorrect. The reading will certainly be different from that of other aircraft which have taken off elsewhere or have been flying for different lengths of time.

Aircraft have been known to collide, or nearly do so, with altimeters reading three or four hundred feet apart. (In aviation, the old ways of measuring heights in feet and distances in nautical miles still prevail.) On long flights, therefore, pilots set their altimeters to the International Standard, adjusting the pressure scale to 1013.2 millibars. They may then be sure that any other aircraft, from different bases and after any time, will be measuring heights in the same way. This is particularly vital when approaching a busy airport and obeying instructions from the ground which are intended to keep airliners safely apart. The true altitude above the ground is unlikely to be the same as that shown on the altimeter. It is important for

As the aircraft rises or descends, the capsule expands or contracts to equalise pressures inside and outside.

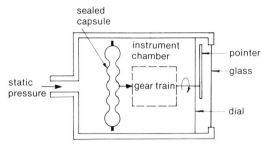

Note: The static pressure opening should be connected to a point on the aircraft where the air pressure is unaffected by speed or turbulence. To find such points is often difficult. In unpressurised aircraft, the interior cabin pressure may be good enough. Otherwise, a static probe tube may be mounted on the wing or nose of the aircraft.

25. Simplified diagram showing how an aircraft altimeter works.

pilots to remember this when flying over high ground in bad weather. It is usual, on arriving above the destination, to re-set the millibar scale to the correct local value before landing, so that the altimeter will read zero when the aircraft lands.

The table (Figure 24) shows some features of the International Standard Atmosphere.

Things to do:

1   Use a *barometer* or barograph to keep a record of changes in air pressure during a day. Compare the pressure readings in millibars that you obtain with those issued by the local weather forecasting office. Suggest reasons for any differences. If possible, take the barometer up to a high place such as a hilltop or the top floor of a tall building, and compare the reading there with that at the lowest place that can be reached.

2   If you can, visit an air traffic control tower, or listen in to air traffic on a suitable (VHF) radio. Notice the information passed to pilots about air pressures, as well as wind speeds and directions. A book about radio procedures and codes can be obtained from government air transport department offices.

3   Try some time-lapse photography of clouds forming and evaporating. This can be done with an ordinary still camera, but more interesting results are obtained with a suitable cine camera. With the still camera, set it up on a firm tripod in a place where the sky can be photographed easily. Watch the clouds for a while before starting, to see which are most likely to produce good pictures, and take note of the wind direction so that the camera will not need to be moved once the photography has been started. Focus at infinity, and when a suitable cloud moves into the viewfinder, take a series of photographs at intervals of half a minute or so. When the photographs are printed, arrange them in the correct order and explain the results. If a (suitably equipped) cine camera is available, arrange for one exposure to be made every second, which, when the film is projected at the normal cine speed, will speed the movement up about thirty times. Other time intervals are also suitable, depending on the effect required.

4   Most introductory courses in physics and general science include experiments to investigate the relationship between gas pressures, volumes and temperatures, and the proportions of oxygen in the air. There are also methods of measuring humidity, air density, mass, etc. Carry out these tests in a laboratory.

Things to find out:

1   Where is it possible, in your district, to obtain a supply of compressed air? How, and at what pressures, is compressed air stored?

2   What is the best pressure for the air in an ordinary bicycle tyre? Why does a bicycle pump become warm when used?

chapter 3

streamlining

When a wind blows against a building, a tree or any other sort of obstacle, there is resistance to the flow of air. The object causing the resistance is fixed in place (unless the forces are so great that it is destroyed), and the air flows.

If a person stands in a wind, the forces can be felt directly (Figure 26). In tornadoes and cyclones people may be pushed over by the wind.

On calm days, or indoors in a gymnasium or indoor athletics stadium, there is no wind. People move through the air and the air resists. Runners can feel this resistance and can even hear the flow rushing past their ears, if they run fast enough. The faster something moves through the air, the greater the air resistance or *drag*. Drag on something moving through the air is the same kind of force as that felt by something standing still with a wind blowing over it. Often both occur together. Cyclists very soon discover this. It is much easier to cycle in the same direction as the wind than into it because the air drag is much more when the wind is against the direction of travel. Sometimes, if the wind is strong, it may be impossible to ride into wind at all because the drag is too much for the cyclist's leg muscles to overcome. On a calm day, the cyclist still feels air drag.

Relative flow

When a vehicle such as a car or large truck moves, there are two ways of thinking about the airflow. Someone standing on the side of the road with measuring instruments is able to feel and measure the way the air behaves as the vehicle rushes by. Some little distance before the vehicle arrives, the air begins to move aside, then it is pushed out of the way altogether as the machine goes by, and behind, there is an inwards movement to fill the space left.

For some distance behind the vehicle, especially if it is a large, fast-moving truck, there is a trailing wake of disturbed air. Dust and litter is swept up and carried along, often being whirled round in the spinning eddies or *vortices* caused by the passage of the truck. Then the air settles down again until the next vehicle disturbs it. All this air movement and turbulence is a sign of drag slowing the movement down, draining energy from the engine and requiring the use of a great deal of fuel if the speed is to be maintained (Figure 27).

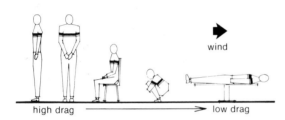

high drag ⟶ low drag

An average human body is shown here in various positions, standing facing the flow, standing sideways to it, sitting, crouching and lying (on a small table). The drag reduces from left to right in the diagram. Try these positions in a wind. Try also the effect of increasing the drag by holding a coat or cloak spread out against the wind.

26. The resistance or 'drag' of any object over which air flows, depends mainly on the size and shape of the object.

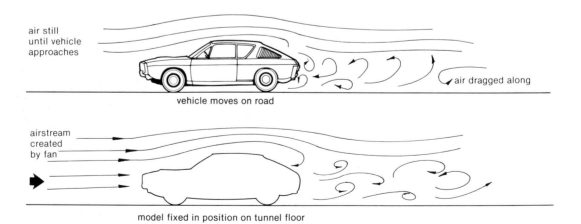

air still until vehicle approaches

air dragged along

vehicle moves on road

airstream created by fan

model fixed in position on tunnel floor

27. Airflow over a moving vehicle compared with flow over a model in a wind tunnel. The pattern of the flow is the same in both cases.

The other way of considering the flow is from the point of view of the driver or a passenger in the vehicle. In this case the air is apparently flowing over the vehicle, just as if it were a wind. There is air drag tending to slow the movement down. The traveller may put a hand out of a window and feel the flow.

It makes very little difference to the pattern and force of the flow whether the object is standing still and the air is blowing past it, or whether the air is still and the object moves through it. A great deal of study and research into the effects of airflow is done in wind tunnels (Figure 28). To test the drag of a new design of car, for example, it would be

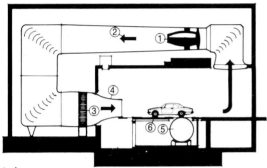

1. fan
2. air duct
3. flow straightener
4. nozzle
5. rotating drum dynamometer
6. rollers to allow wheels to turn

28. How a wind tunnel is arranged.

very difficult to run the vehicle along the road and try to measure the drag. All the instruments would have to ride along with the car, the scientists would have to be moving along with it too, either inside or following in another vehicle. If there was any wind this would upset the measurements. Instead, what is usually done is to make a model of the vehicle and fix it in a wind tunnel. The large fan in the tunnel creates an artificial airflow over the model which is just the same as the flow over the car when it moves through calm air. The instruments can all be fixed outside the tunnel and the observers can make accurate measurements easily. It is also easier to alter the shape to try to improve the drag figures. A wind tunnel model can be changed in any way required between the tests, without requiring real wheels, engine or any of the other things needed for a vehicle to move on a road.

Trying to travel faster

In the days of horse-drawn carriages and carts, air drag was not very important because the speed of travel was slow. The first really fast vehicles were railway trains. When these began to reach speeds of 100 km/h and more (which was very common in the later 19th century), air drag became more noticeable. It was found that the drag increased in proportion to the square of the speed of the airflow. The Bernoulli *Square Law* applied. If the speed of the airflow over the train was doubled, the drag increased by four times. When a train moved at 15 km/h, it met some air resistance but this was unimportant compared with the friction of the wheels in their bearings and the resistance from the track. If the speed rose to 30 km/h, air resistance was four times greater than before, but still not very serious. As speeds doubled again, and then again, engineers soon realised that air drag was becoming very large indeed. A train going at 150 km/h meets not ten times, but a hundred times the air drag that it has to cope with at 15 km/h. One way of dealing with such forces was to increase the power of the locomotives used to pull the trains. They became bigger. Unfortunately they also became very heavy, costly to build and used huge quantities of fuel.

At last people began to study airflow and discover ways of reducing drag. Streamlined trains began to appear, which went faster with the same, or even less, power (Figures 31 and 32). The only way to counteract the effects of the Square Law of drag was to improve the air flow over the vehicle.

29 The first vehicles to travel fast enough for air drag to show its effects were steam-driven railway trains, pulled by locomotives such as this 'G 1'. No attempt was made to smooth the airflow. As the speed rose higher, the cost of fuel increased greatly. (Australian National Railways)

30   The 'Overland Express', which runs from Melbourne to Adelaide daily, shows how attention has been given to streamlining on modern trains. In Britain, France, and Japan special high-speed trains have been in use for some years, with a streamlined form far superior to this, and capable of much greater speeds. (Australian National Railways)

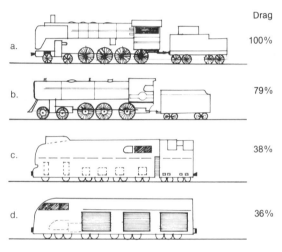

a. steam engine with smoke-deflector plates and coal tender
b. steam engine without deflector plates
c. streamlined steam locomotive with tender
d. streamlined diesel locomotive
Reductions in drag of more than 60 per cent may be achieved by streamlining.

31. The drag of railway locomotives.

The same sort of thing happened with cars. At first these were truly horseless carriages. They looked like coaches and moved hardly any faster. Air drag was not important. Soon, speeds began to increase. When racing cars began to appear, bigger and bigger engines were made to go faster still. The early record-breaking cars were often very big and heavy, becoming almost uncontrollable because of their huge mass. To make them turn safely on a racing track became nearly impossible (Figure 33).

As with trains, ways of reducing air drag were sought. It became possible to go faster with a 'low-drag' body on the vehicle, even if the engine was less powerful (Figure 34).

Today, it is realised more than ever that air drag is important. An ordinary family car which is badly shaped will use more fuel than one which is correctly designed for low drag.

Wind tunnel tests, originally done for aircraft rather than land vehicles, soon showed that the best shape for low drag was different

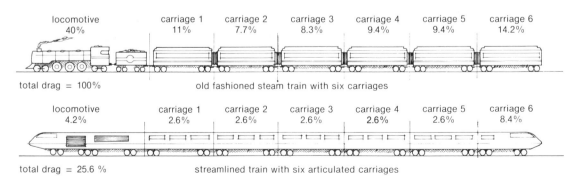

Can you explain why the last carriage creates more drag than the ones in the middle?

32. Comparison of drag of whole trains.

from that expected. Many people believed that the lowest drag would come from a shape that was pointed at the front, to cut through the air, and it was thought that the shape at the rear end would not make much difference. This turned out to be quite incorrect. If the rear is wrongly shaped, the airflow will separate. The separated flow creates a great deal of drag as the car pulls a very large, turbulent wake behind it. The best shape, giving the least drag, is one which allows the flow to remain streamlined. This requires a fairly long, pointed tail, with a smoothly rounded front end (Figure 35).

Even today, cars generally do not have this shape. This is because they have to contain people, in comfortable seats, with a clear view of the road. The engine has to be cooled, space must be available for luggage and so on (Figure 36). There are often roof racks, radio aerials, bumper bars and wing mirrors, all of which may be very necessary, but which upset the streamlining. Even so, the best modern cars are very much better, aerodynamically, than the older ones (Figures 37, 38 and Photo 39).

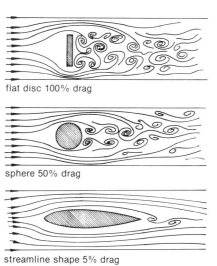

flat disc 100% drag

sphere 50% drag

streamline shape 5% drag

35. The drag of various solid bodies.

1. General flow and drag: fuel economy and speed are affected.

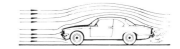

2. Interior airflow for ventilation: where should the air intake and exit be placed?

3. Engine cooling: will there be enough airflow to cool the engine at all times?

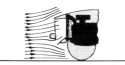

4. Safety: will the car tend to pitch badly or lift off the road at high speeds or in rough winds?

36. Four types of aerodynamic problem for a car designer.

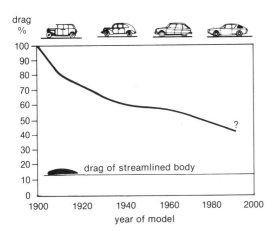

What should the shape of cars be in the future?

33. How the air drag of cars has changed over the years, taking a 1900 'horseless carriage' as 100%.

A well-streamlined car also designed to avoid taking off at very high speeds.

34. Donald Campbell's record-breaking car.

To streamline a heavy transport vehicle is hard. The loads carried are usually the wrong shape and the rear end is nearly always cut off rather suddenly. The turbulent flow behind such a vehicle is very commonly felt; the air is pulled along behind the truck as an extra, although invisible, load. The engine has to move not only the cargo and the vehicle itself, but a large mass of air as well. The disturbed flow is often enough to shake other, smaller vehicles as the truck passes. Some small improvements have been made at the front, on some heavy vehicles (Photo 40). Carefully shaped plates may be used to

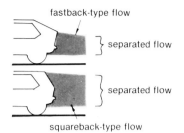

If flow separation behind the car can be reduced, savings of fuel and higher speeds are possible.

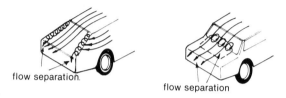

37. Quite small changes in car body shape can make large differences to the drag.

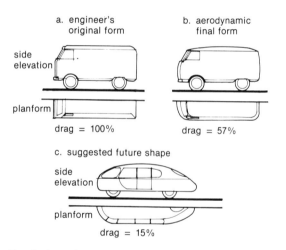

The planform of a vehicle is its shape when viewed from directly above or below.

38. How the drag of the VW Kombi van was reduced by rounding off the corners.

smooth the airflow over the top of the driving cab and the front end of the load. This makes quite a worthwhile saving in fuel. The same idea can assist the towing of a caravan trailer behind an ordinary car.

In road trains where several large trailers follow behind the prime mover, the air drag of the train is somewhat less than it would be for several separate trucks of the same size. The trailers are in the wake of the first part of the train, and gain some reduction in total drag. The same thing applies to railway trains

39   Research into the best streamlined form for a motor car goes on all over the world. Here is shown a wind tunnel model of a car designed by the Italian firm *Pininfarina*. The numerous wool tufts will show how the airflow passes over the vehicle during testing. Measurements showed that the drag of this shape was less than half that of a typical family saloon car of the same size, and the fuel saving would be 15 per cent. (*Pininfarina*)

40   It is very difficult to streamline a modern, heavy, load-carrying vehicle, since the load is usually a large, rectangular box shape. The first photograph shows the airflow in a smoke tunnel as it is pushed up and over the driver's cab and then the trailer.

Some improvement can be made if the airflow is smoothed over the front of the vehicle. In the second photograph the model semi-trailer has been fitted with a carefully shaped deflector above the cab, to help the air to pass smoothly, without separation, to the top of the load. A wing-like aerofoil is also used above the windscreen to assist the flow to curve around the sharp angle there. This is very similar to the wing slots sometimes fitted on aeroplanes to delay stalling. (Woolcock Enterprises)

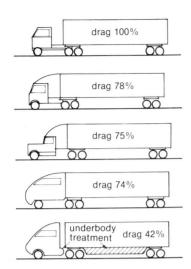

Worthwhile improvements can be made by shaping the driver's cab, but the load cannot be shaped for smooth flow.

41. Streamlining a large semi-trailer with load.

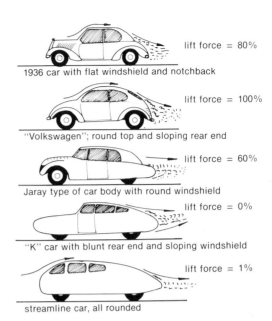

42. Cars which lift themselves into the air.

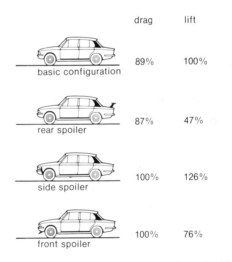

43. Spoilers to hold the car down can reduce the lift forces but may increase the drag.

with many carriages. In addition, high speed trains are carefully shaped in every detail. Everything possible is done to keep the airflow smooth. Windows are made flush with the outer skins of the carriages, door handles are recessed, the front of the locomotive is smoothly rounded and the last coach tapers off to a point.

Cars which take off

There is a difficulty about streamlined road vehicles, which arises because of Bernoulli's theorem about flow speeds and pressures. A fast airflow over a smoothly curved body causes a reduction of pressure where the flow is fastest. This creates a lifting force similar to that which can carry a roof off a building. Some small cars which were designed before this was realised would tend to 'take off', being lifted off the road by the reduction in pressure above (Figure 42). This was especially likely if they were travelling fast in windy conditions, when the airspeed was increased by occasional heavy gusts. One solution, still sometimes used, is to fit 'flow spoilers' which break the streamlines and increase the pressure (Figure 43). Racing cars may be fitted with wing-shaped surfaces, turned upside down to push the wheels onto the road. This is still done sometimes but it tends to increase the drag and slow the car down.

Racing cars now make use of Bernoulli's theorem in a way that helps them to stay firmly on the road. When the car moves, air flows underneath as well as above. If the bottom of the car is correctly shaped, it can be made to act like a pipe, or tunnel, with a narrow section in which the flow speed increases.

As Bernoulli discovered long ago, in such a narrowing channel, the air pressure falls and on a fast car, it can be made to drop even lower than the pressure above. There is then a powerful force holding the car down; the

44   The Formula Pacific car, driven by Bruce Allison, shows how aerodynamics may be used. The wing-like shapes ahead of the front wheels, and the large aerofoil at the rear, act like aeroplane wings upside down, the 'lift' force produced by them pushing the car more firmly onto the road. Under the car, between the side plates or 'skirts', the Bernoulli effect creates even more down-load. (Murray Scott)

The angles of the front and rear aerofoils or 'wings' may be adjusted to give the required steering and cornering characteristics to suit the particular track and driver.

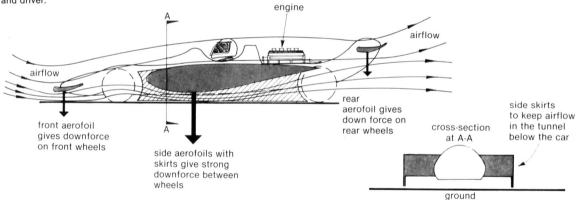

45. The aerodynamics of a racing car.

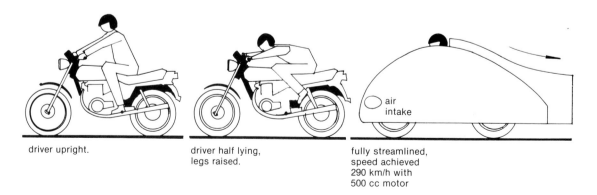

46. How the drag of a motor cycle might be reduced.

faster it goes, the more powerful the Bernoulli effect (Figure 45). It becomes possible to drive much faster without being lifted off the road. At the same time, because the flow under the car, as well as above it, is streamlined, there is less drag. Many cars are quite well streamlined above and on the sides, but underneath there are projections and other awkward shapes which the air cannot follow smoothly.

Things to do:

1   On a calm day, or in a gymnasium, run as fast as possible and listen to the airflow, and feel the air drag. Try running with a large piece of cardboard held flat in front. What happens if the cardboard is held edgewise? Try holding it at different angles to the flow. At some angles it will tend to push sideways one way or another; at other angles it will tend to lift or to push down.

2   Take a bicycle to a good open space such as a schoolyard, and ride it against the wind. Then ride downwind. If it is not very windy, it should be possible to ride with the wind and find a speed at which there is no air drag (except that the wheel spokes will always create some). Explain how this occurs. Try different bicycles with different shaped handlebars. Why do some bicycles have dropped handlebars?

3   Attach several small streamers, such as tufts of wool or strips of light cloth, to a car, using water-soluble gum. As a passenger in the car, watch the way the tufts or streamers move as the car travels. What does the flow do just ahead of the windscreen? How does it behave behind the car? Try to find out if there are any regions of separated flow. (Afterwards, remove the streamers and clean the car!)

4   Make a simple wind tunnel similar to that shown in Figure 47 to test different shapes for their drag. A smoke generator like that in Figure 48 may be made to show how the airflow moves.

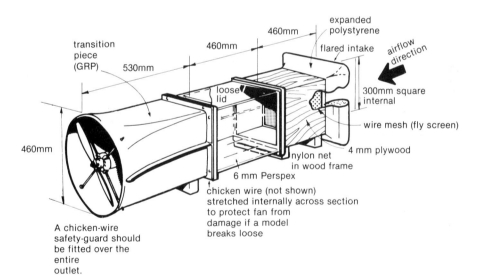

Multi-purpose wind tunnel

The tunnel was designed at Lanchester Polytechnic (UK), as a portable unit which could be constructed in a short time from a variety of materials. The sectionalised design enables a number of groups of students to be involved in the construction at the same time.

The use of a single 0.4m propeller driven by a spin-drier motor fed via 'Variac' makes it possible to run the tunnel at low or high speeds.

The tunnel is therefore suitable for flow visualisation using a smoke comb for measurements of lift and drag using a suitable balance,

Access to the working area is obtained through the top of the tunnel which is closed by a Perspex lid. This lid can be used to support a balance where necessary.

At low speeds the flow is smoothed using a screen of nylon net or wire gauze, and the introduction of smoke will show the streamlining around various obstacles such as aerofoils and model cars. Work can also be done on wind patterns around buildings. With suitable lighting, photographs of the smoke trails can be produced. For high speeds suitable for measuring lift and drag on aerofoils, the smoothing screen is removed.

47. A simple wind tunnel which may be built to experiment with airflow over model cars, buildings, aircraft, etc.

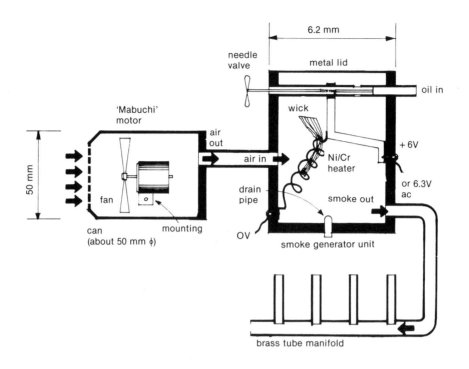

Smoke generator

This generator, developed at Lanchester Polytechnic (UK), consists of three separate units: blower, smoke generator and smoke comb. The units are connected together by flexible tubes, and a valve at the blower outlet allows regulation of the airflow to the generator.

Blower

A small electric motor fitted with a sheet metal or wooden fan is mounted centrally into an open-ended can. A short length of copper tube is connected to the closed end of the can to provide an outlet for the air.

Smoke generator

A Perspex box contains the apparatus for producing a smoke from an oil. The oil into the box is directed onto a wick and the rate of flow is controlled by means of a needle valve. The wick is supported near a Ni/Cr heater coil. The electrical connections to the coil are carried out through the sides of the box to terminals suitable for 6V supply. Tubes for air, smoke and drain connections are fitted through the side of the box in the positions shown.

Smoke comb

A number of 18 gauge bore brass or copper tubes are soldered at right angles to a larger supply tube. The number and spacing of the 18 gauge tubes will depend on the particular tunnel and application.

48. A smoke generator and smoke comb which may be used in the wind tunnel to show airflow patterns.

Things to find out:

1   How does the need to cool the engine tend to spoil the airflow around a car?

2   How was the speed record for bicycles established?

3   What are the speed records for the various kinds of land vehicle? Find pictures of these vehicles, and study them. How have the shapes changed over the years? Suggest reasons for these changes. (Not all the changes were concerned with drag reduction.)

4   In the early days of fast railway trains, sometimes the coaches of two trains passing one another on separate tracks would lean towards one another and smash together. The engineers could not understand this at first because at slow speeds there was apparently plenty of room to spare between the trains. Can you explain what was happening?

5   Water flow is often very similar to airflow. What happens if two ships sail side by side, close together?

chapter 4

sailing

It is not known when or where the first sailing boats were made. It may have been in Egypt at the time of the first great Pharaohs, or in China or Persia. Quite probably the idea was thought of in several different places at about the same time. Boatmen rowing or paddling along rivers such as the Nile, the Yangtze or the Euphrates found it hard work to go upstream against the current, but they felt the force of the wind on their vessels, and knew that the effort needed was less if the air was moving along the way they wished to go. Perhaps someone set up a canopy or an awning to keep the sun off, and saw the wind catching it and the rowers being helped by it. Not long afterwards the first true sail may have been put up — just a mat woven from reeds, set up on a pole. When the wind was favourable the sail helped to push the boat along but if the wind changed, or the boat had to travel the other way, the sail had to come down.

Running before the wind

It is easy to understand how such a simple sail helps to drive a boat (Figure 49). Land vehicles can be provided with sails in the same way and will sail, providing there is a suitable surface for them to move along. The wind strikes the sail and is slowed down, creating an area of high pressure on the side facing the flow. On the other side the flow separates and the pressure tends to return to more or less the normal value. There is a difference in pressure between the two sides of the sail. This provides the driving force.

The kind of flow is very like that near a tall building, with a region of separated flow

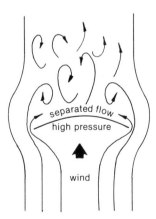

49. Airflow round a simple sail when running dead downwind.

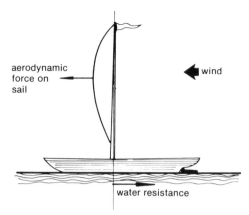

When the aerodynamic thrust force equals the water resistance, the ship will maintain a steady speed.

Note: The pressure on the sail will also tend to push the ship's bows down.

50. Forces acting on a sailing ship.

behind and a trailing wake. This separated flow region explains why several sails, arranged one behind the other, did not work very well when first tried. The second sail was in the wake of the first. For this reason, most of the earliest sailing ships had only one large, more or less square sail fixed in the simplest way across the ship and not easily changed in setting.

There are some obvious limitations with such sails. They need the wind behind them to gain any driving force from it. Even when going along with the wind right behind (this is called *running* 'dead' *before the wind*), they cannot sail any faster than the wind itself. In gentle breezes this means very slow movement. If the wind is blowing at, say, 10 km/h, and the boat being driven by it is moving at 5 km/h, the sailors will actually feel a breeze of only 5 km/h across the deck, blowing from behind towards the bow of their ship. If the ship speeds up through the water, to 7 km/h, the sailors notice an apparent drop in the wind speed. Since the vessel is going at 7 km/h, there is only a 3 km/h wind across the deck. The pressures on the sail depend, not on the true wind velocity across the water, but on the speed of the breeze that blows relative to the ship. When running dead before the wind, this relative or apparent wind gets less as the ship sails faster. If the ship ever actually reached the same speed as the wind there would be no relative wind at all on the deck and the sail would hang limply, giving no driving force. The ship would slow down because of the resistance of the water. When the driving force from the sail equals the resistance force from the water, the ship moves at a steady rate, always at some speed less than the wind (Figure 50). This condition, with the resistance of the water equal to the driving or thrust force from the sail, is a state of equilibrium. The vessel will continue to move at a steady speed until there is some change of the forces acting on it. Anyone who has sailed in a yacht or who has learned wind-surfing soon finds this out in practice. Even if the size of the sail is increased greatly, as in the *spinnakers* used on racing yachts, the wind speed is the limit when running dead downwind. Bigger sails may help the boat to get closer to this speed, but the closer the boat gets to the true wind velocity, the less the relative wind blowing on the sail and so the less the driving force becomes.

It was not long before the earliest sailors discovered they could get some help from the breeze even if they did not wish to run dead before it. When they needed to steer at an angle, perhaps to follow curves in the river they were navigating, they used a steering oar or steerboard to point the ship the way they wished to go, and by changing the angle of the sail across the vessel, it was possible to keep the sail full. It was probably when this discovery was made that ships began to be built with masts supporting cross booms to carry the sail. The boom could be swung around to either side at an angle, the ropes at the sail's lower corners (called sheets) being adjusted accordingly. They also found, prob-ably to their dismay, that the ship tended to heel over sideways when sailing in this way. To keep it more or less upright, ballast and a keel were added.

Resolving forces

How a sail, set at an angle to the ship, can drive it, is explained by *resolution of the forces* on the sail (Figure 51).

Any force whatever can be imagined as being two separate forces acting in such a way that they have the same effect as the original force. To drive the ship, a force is needed along the direction of movement, that is, from the stern towards the bow, depen-ding on the direction the steersman decides. The sail is set at an angle so the simple force on the sail can be resolved into two: one driv-ing the ship forward, and the other pushing sideways. The proportion of the sail force

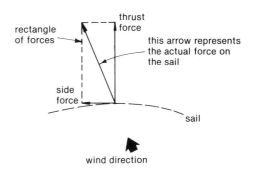

The wind thrust on the sail may be 'resolved' into two forces: one which drives the ship in the desired direction; the other causes it to heel over and move sideways in the water (leeway).

51. Resolution of forces.

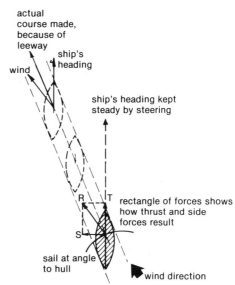

Note: The helmsman must allow for leeway.

52. By correct setting of sail, a ship may make its course at an angle to the wind.

which is useful, driving forward, will depend on the sail's angle. The other part of the force, resolved, will cause the boat to heel over and will also tend to push it sideways through the water. This sideways movement is called *leeway* (Figure 52).

To resolve the forces correctly, it is necessary to complete the rectangle of forces. The diagonal of the rectangle is an arrow drawn to a scale to represent both the strength and direction of the sail force. The centre line of the ship gives the direction of the resolved thrust and the heeling force is at right angles to this.

Trim and balance

It was soon found that some ships were easier to manage than others. The reason was the position of the sail, and its mast, on the ship. If the sail was far forward, the part of the wind force resolved sideways tended to force the bow of the ship round away from the wind, providing the steersman with a severe struggle (Figure 53a). The steerboard or rudder had to be turned to a large angle against the water flow, requiring much force.

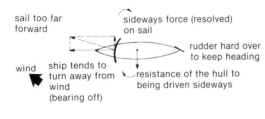

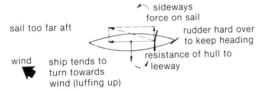

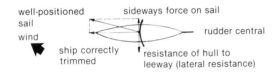

53. Trim and balance.

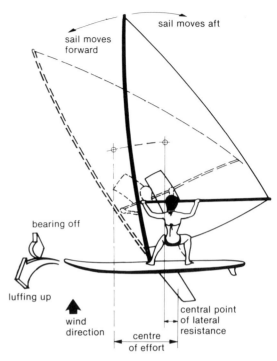

A sailboard is steered by raking the sail forward — to bear away from the wind and aft, to luff up into the wind.

54. Steering a sailboard.

This also tended to slow down the ship. If the sail and mast were too far aft, the opposite happened (Figure 53b): the ship would constantly try to turn into the wind. If the sail could be placed somewhere nearer the middle of the ship, a balanced or nearly balanced position could be found and the rudder would hardly be needed at all, once the angle of the sail was set correctly for the direction. To achieve this balance or trim was often very difficult. The centre of effort or *centre of pressure* on the sail had to be brought as nearly as possible above the centre of sideways or lateral resistance of the hull in the water. Only then was it possible to steer a large ship with a small rudder (Figure 53c).

In windsurfing, the small keel or dagger board provides most of the lateral resistance.

55   The simplest form of sailing vessel, the boardsailer. Note how the masthead pennant streams to the side, showing the wind direction relative to the board, which is moving rapidly towards the camera. To counteract the sideways heeling force, Sue Ford has to lean to the windward side. (Adelaide *Advertiser*)

The sailboard is steered without a rudder by moving the sail's centre of pressure forward or aft (Figure 54). When the centre of pressure is forward, ahead of the dagger board, the sailboard turns away from the wind, and when the centre of pressure is moved aft, the board turns towards the wind. To keep straight, the two centres must be above one another. The smallest movement of the sail causes a turn. The sailboard is easily upset by changes of wind or water, and requires constant trimming.

Larger ships with longer hulls can be trimmed to sail steadily in a straight line without the necessity to move the rudder much.

Beating against the wind

The next great discovery probably came almost as an accident. When a sail is running before the wind, the airflow around it separates (Figure 56a). It was found that sometimes, at certain angles of the relative wind, the sail would give much greater drive. Although the sailors did not at first understand why it happened, the reason was that the flow over a sail, when set at a small angle to the relative wind, becomes streamlined. The greater force is a result of the increased speed of flow on the outer side of the sail. The pressure there is reduced in accordance with Bernoulli's theorem, and the difference in pressure between the two surfaces of the sail is much greater (Figure 56c). The effect is almost exactly the same as that which causes low-pitched house roofs to be lifted off in gales. It is necessary to set the sail at the correct angle. What counts is not the angle of the sail to the hull, but its angle to the airflow. This angle is called the *angle of attack*. If it is too small, there is little drive and the sail flaps uselessly (Figure 56d). If the angle to the wind is too large, the airflow cannot follow the curve of the canvas (Figure 56b) and the sail *stalls*; it still gives some driving force but not as much as when it is set at the best angle of attack to the wind.

It was soon found possible to sail across the wind, on what is called a *reach*, and even, with a well trimmed sail and a good hull, to *beat against the wind* at an angle (Figure 57). Progress can be made against the wind by *tacking*, that is, beating in one direction first, then *going about* to the other tack, and so making headway in a zig-zag. It was this important development that made regular ocean voyages possible for sailing ships.

It was also now possible to set up more sails on several masts one behind the other. Because the relative wind was nearly always passing over the ship at an angle instead of coming directly from aft, the flow could pass between the various sets of sails smoothly,

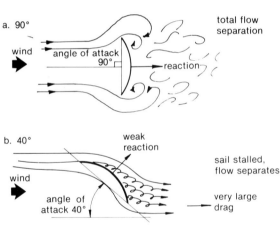

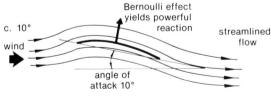

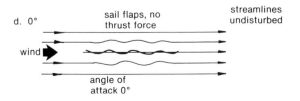

56. Airflow over sails at different angles of attack.

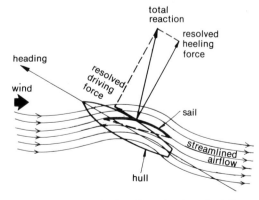

57. How a sailing yacht is able to beat against the wind.

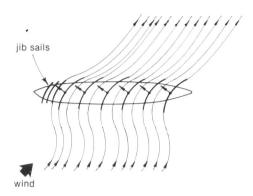

jib sails

wind

Providing the sails are set correctly at angles of attack which do not cause stalling (flow separation), many sails may be carried by a single ship. The 'square-rigged' and 'schooner-rigged' clippers were designed in this way.

58. Setting of multiple sails.

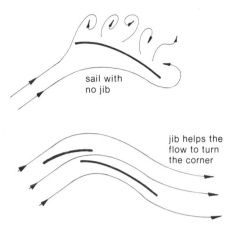

sail with no jib

jib helps the flow to turn the corner

A modern yacht may use its jib sail to keep the flow over the main sail streamlined.

60. Use of a jib sail.

59   One of the great clippers, square-rigged sailing ships that used to voyage regularly across all the oceans. Note that the sails are carefully trimmed to the angle which gives the best forward thrust, without one set of sails masking another. The ship is the *Pamir*. (Source unknown)

and the wake of one sail did not interfere with the others (Figure 58).

It is also possible to use one sail to help another. The small, triangular jib sails on modern sailing vessels help the airflow to curve round onto the main sail when, without such help, the larger sail would stall (Figure 60).

Aeroplane wings often use this effect, with a small wing or slat which opens just ahead of the mainplane if there is any chance of stalling. By these improvements to the sails and by shaping the hulls to allow faster movement through the water while, at the same time, increasing the lateral resistance, sailing ships became much faster and more reliable. It was soon discovered also that a sail set along the ship's centre line instead of crosswise, would provide just as much driving force, so lateen- and schooner-rigged ships appeared, and barques which had square and schooner-rigged sails used together. Modern yachts are nearly always rigged fore-and-aft, except when running with the wind under the spinnaker.

When sailing on a *reach*, across the wind, the driving forces from the sails are very large and ships are able to move a good deal faster than the wind. It also helps to have tall masts carrying sails as high as possible, but a tall ship tends to heel over more dangerously. Sailors were the first to realise that the driving force from a sail had to be obtained with as little drag as possible. On the old sailing ships, there was a great deal of rigging, tall masts and yardarms, numerous ropes, tackle blocks and stays, all of which created drag and increased leeway and heeling.

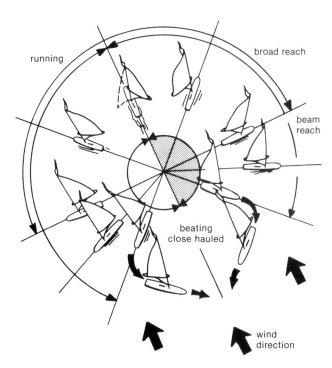

Some sailing vessels can sail 'closer to the wind' than others, but none can make headway directly against the wind. Progress in this direction requires tacking.

61. The points of sailing.

The aspect ratio

Another important point was the spilling of the air from the top and bottom edges of the square sails. This not only decreased the thrust, but caused extra drag. To reduce all these losses, tall, narrow sails were introduced (Figure 62).

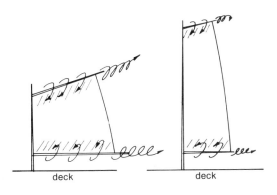

At the upper and lower edges of a sail, the air tends to spill from the high pressure side to the low. A tall, narrow sail is less affected.

62. Air-spill from sails with different aspect ratios.

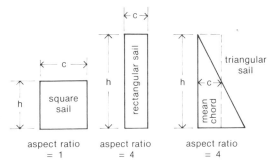

The areas of all three sails are equal.

63. Aspect ratio.

The height of a sail in relation to its area is expressed as a ratio, called the *aspect ratio* (Figure 63). A perfectly square sail, with its width exactly equal to its height, has an aspect ratio of one. A rectangular-shaped sail that is twice as tall as it is wide has an aspect ratio of two. One that is four times as tall as it is wide, has an aspect ratio of four, and so on. In working out this ratio for other shapes, the average width of the sail is used. A triangular sail has the width measured half way up when the aspect ratio is worked out. If the sail has curved edges, as most do, the average width may be found by dividing the total area by the height. The figure found by this calculation is usually called the mean *chord* of the surface.

Sailing vessels of various kinds are still widely used in South-east Asia, and in many other regions for training and of course for sport. The high cost of fuels for motor-driven ships has encouraged some shipowners to think of returning to sailing ships for carrying large cargoes. Much is known now about air-flow over sails, and it should be possible to build a very efficient rig. With modern methods of predicting weather and wind using satellite transmissions of weather patterns, sailors should be able to find the wind required to keep the ship moving and avoid the long calms which used sometimes to trap the older clippers that voyaged regularly across the oceans.

Things to do:

1   Make a model yacht or land yacht, and test it with different types of sail (Figure 64 and Photo 67).

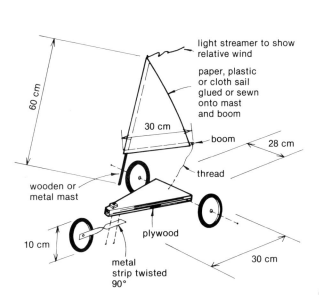

light streamer to show relative wind

paper, plastic or cloth sail glued or sewn onto mast and boom

60 cm

30 cm

boom

28 cm

thread

wooden or metal mast

10 cm

plywood

30 cm

metal strip twisted 90°

Use rubber wheels for best results. The dimensions are not very critical.

64. A simple land yacht model.

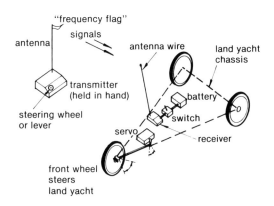

"frequency flag"

signals

antenna

antenna wire

land yacht chassis

transmitter (held in hand)

battery

steering wheel or lever

switch

servo

receiver

front wheel steers land yacht

Radio controls may be fitted to the land yacht model. The front wheel must be made steerable. With additional control gear it is also possible to change the sail trim.

65. Controls for a model land yacht.

66. A full-sized land yacht.

67   To make a small land yacht is very easy. The students here are adjusting the setting of the sail before allowing the yacht to move. The sail is made from a plastic rubbish bin liner, and the wheels may be purchased cheaply from hardware or rubber stores. (Author)

2   On a model yacht or land yacht, attach a light streamer (tissue paper or woollen thread) to the masthead. When the boat is sailing, observe the direction of the streamer relative to the boat. If you are able to go sailing or board sailing, use a streamer or small pennant in the same way. Try sailing in different directions and observe the angle of the streamer to the sail in each case.

3   Visit a yacht club or model yacht club and learn about the trimming and steering of yachts. (Model yachts are often sailed under radio control.)

Things to find out:

1   What are the main types of rig for sailing ships and what are the advantages of each type?

2   What are the main classes of yachts used for racing? How do they differ from one another?

3   What are the advantages and disadvantages of the catamaran type of sailing vessel?

4   What are modern racing sails made from? Who makes them?

chapter 5

power from
the wind

The first windmills, so far as is known, were built in China several thousand years ago, and were used for pumping water. Corn grinding mills were used in Persia, also from very early times — the exact dates are not certain.

The early Chinese windmills had paddle wheels with wooden blades or sails of matting arranged round the central spindle. Each paddle was hinged with stops placed so that it resisted the wind as it moved round one side of the centre but trailed freely as it came round the other side (Figure 68).

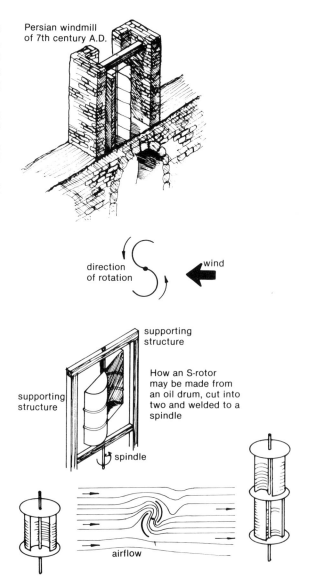

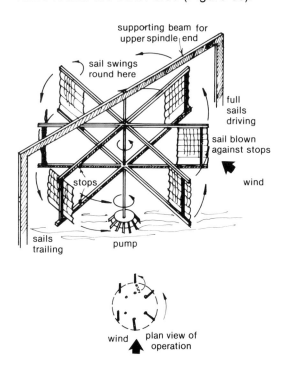

Note: Only two or three sails are full at any time. In an actual mill, additional bracing members are required.

68. Schematic diagram of ancient Chinese windmill used for pumping water.

The improved Savonius rotor, which may also be doubled up to even out the power flow.

69. The Savonius rotor.

The Persian mills usually had paddles fixed rigidly to the spindle. The wind was then directed onto just one side of the mill by means of walls and screens. Such mills were built on towers with the millstones below. The mills were set up to take advantage of the most common winds in their district. Various improvements were made. The mill tower could be made taller, because the wind above the ground tends to be faster. Near the ground the air is slowed down a great deal by friction. It became possible to work the mill in several different winds by a simple system

of wooden shutters to close off one channel and open another. To stop the mill, when there was no grinding to be done, or to allow repair work, the shutters could be closed off altogether. If the wind was very strong the mill could be damaged if allowed to turn too fast, so it was important to have a means of shutting it off.

A more up-to-date version is the Savonius turbine, which needs no artificial channels or gates and will turn in a wind from any direction (Figure 69). This type of rotor was invented in 1921 by S.J. Savonius, and it is sometimes known as the *S rotor* because the blades make the shape of the letter S when viewed from above. One of the greatest advantages of this type of windmill is that it can be made very easily by people who lack advanced technical skills or who cannot obtain much in the way of materials. An oil drum may be cut into two halves, vertically, and the two sections welded onto the spindle, which may be an old axle from a scrapped road vehicle. Set up vertically in suitable bearings, such a rotor will drive a small electric generator (which may also come from a scrapped vehicle), and can provide enough power for a small water pump, or, by charging a set of car batteries, a radio or a small electric light. If the wind dies, the batteries continue to provide power for some time.

The simple S rotor turns because there is a difference in drag between the blade which presents its outer or convex side to the wind, and the side which faces the wind with its concave side. In the same way as a ship running dead before the wind, the rotor blade cannot move any faster than the wind which pushes it, and there is resistance at all times from the other blade which has to be driven against the flow. An improvement is made if the two blades are separated slightly, leaving a gap between them. Both blades then act, during part of their rotation, like the sails of a ship in a side wind, and Bernoulli's theorem operates. The airflow becomes streamlined and flows over the outer sides of the blades, causing a reduction of air pressure. The flow continues through the gap or slot between the blades, and flows over the other blade with the streamlines curving in the other direction. This causes a favourable pressure change on the other blade too. Unfortunately the power obtained from such a rotor is rather uneven. The blades continually change their angle of attack to the airflow and as they turn, at some point in each rotation, the flow breaks down and the rotor stalls until the blade gets into a better position again. To even out the fluctuations of power, it is possible to set up two or more rotors one above the other on the same spindle, with the blades at different angles so that when one set is stalled the others are still driving powerfully. Some modern wind turbines are based on this principle. It is possible to improve the S rotor still further by channelling the airflow with guiding vanes and shutters.

The European windmill

News of windmills probably travelled to western Europe during the time of the Crusades. Windmills began to appear in the west about 1100 A.D. but the European mills that developed were of a different type, with long, narrow sails on a spindle facing into the wind.

A model of such a turbine may be made very simply from a twisted strip of thin metal pivoted at its centre on an axle. To understand exactly how the air drives it round is somewhat more difficult.

If the sails or blades of the rotor are set at an angle to the airflow, with the spindle pointing directly into the wind, the mill will begin to turn. The sail produces the driving force in exactly the same way as the sail of a ship set at a small angle of attack to the wind (Figure 71). The flow is streamlined, and a difference in pressure is created between the two sides, producing an aerodynamic reaction force. As with the ship's sail, this force

70   A Dutch windmill, one of many thousands that once were used for pumping water and grinding grain. Note the twist in each sail to achieve the correct pitch as the rotor turns. The fantail rotor of this mill is near ground level. It turns its wheels along a circular track, moving the upper part of the mill to face the wind.

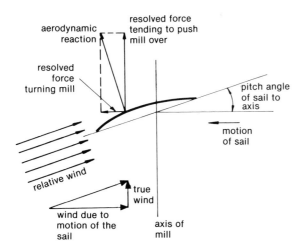

71. Why a windmill sail turns.

may be resolved into two: one driving the rotor round, the other — the drag force — tending to push the entire mill away in the downwind direction. This is similar to the drag forces causing leeway and heeling in ships.

As soon as the mill begins to turn, the direction of the airflow relative to the turning sail changes. This is the same kind of effect as that on a sailing ship when it is under way. The wind felt by sailors on deck is the relative wind, which combines the motion of the ship with the true wind so that the actual flow of air over them, and over the sails, is different from the wind felt by someone on the land. The moving sails of a windmill, in much the same way, feel a relative wind which combines their motion with the true wind (Figure 71).

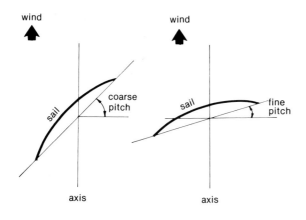

72. Coarse and fine pitch.

For each angle of setting of the blades of the rotor, there will be a particular speed at which rotation will settle down. A rotor which has its blades set almost at right angles to the flow will be stalled completely at first, but once rotation starts, it will spin very rapidly. A rotor with blades set at a coarse angle or coarse *pitch*, will begin to turn very easily but will never go very fast (Figure 72).

The early millers in Europe had no means of changing the pitch of the sails on their mills. They set them at an angle which gave good results most of the time, but in light winds they could not work at all, and in very strong winds they tended to run much too fast and would break up. If the mill was loaded with heavy grindstones, the rate of rotation was reduced.

Another very important feature of such wind *turbines* is that the inner parts of the sail or blade travel a much smaller distance as they turn than the outer tips. For example, many old windmills had a diameter, from the tip of one sail to the tip opposite, of about 20 metres. One blade then had a span of 10 metres. During one rotation, the distance moved by the extreme tip is found by the formula which relates the circumference of a circle to its radius (Figure 73). This is:

Circumference = 2 × 3.142 × Radius

With a sail of 10 metres span, the tip travels 62.84 metres during each revolution. Halfway out along the vane, the distance travelled is halved and near the centre, at one metre from the spindle of the rotor, the sail moves through only 6.284 m, one tenth of the distance at the tip. This difference changes the *relative flow* direction at each point on the mill blade. If the blade is set at the same pitch all the way along, it is likely to be stalled in some places while other parts of it are driving well. To make the entire sail drive efficiently, the pitch should be changed gradually by giving the vane a twist along its length. The pitch at the root, or inner end, should be coarser than that near the tips. The best of the European windmills, which appeared in the eighteenth and nineteenth centuries, were built in this way; each sail having a definite twist from root to tip.

The fantail rotor

To keep the rotor facing into the wind, it is necessary to turn the mill round as the wind

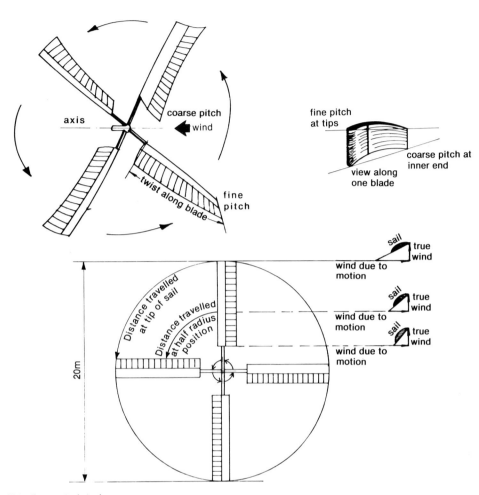

73. Why windmill sails are twisted.

varies. In the earliest mills, this was done by hand. The miller had to watch for any change of the weather, and used various systems of levers and gear wheels to rotate the whole upper part of the mill tower.

Later, a device called the *fantail* rotor was invented. This was a small set of sails behind the main rotor, with its axis of rotation at right angles. It was connected to gears which turned the mill (Figure 74). If the wind changed, the fantail automatically began to spin, one way or the other, depending on which direction the wind now came from. The gearing was such that the main rotor would always turn to face the new direction and the fantail would stop turning as soon as this position was reached.

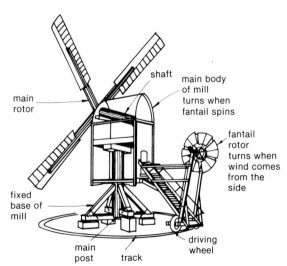

In this type of mill, the main part of the mill, carrying the rotor on its shaft, turns to face the wind whenever the fantail rotor spins. A smooth circular track is required for the driving wheels to run on. In other types of mill, only the upper section or head of the mill turns, with the fantail mounted higher.

74. A post mill with fantail.

Speed control

A serious problem with all windmills is controlling the speed. To stop the mill turning altogether, either when there is no work to be done, or when repairs are necessary, the rotor may be turned out of the wind. Many earlier mills had canvas sails which could be reefed like the sails of a ship. Others were equipped with slatted vanes like a modern venetian blind. These could be set at different angles to let more or less air escape through the sail. In very strong winds such devices could also be used for speed control.

In modern times, much work is being done to improve windmills, to use them for power generation. Using aerodynamic knowledge, with metals and plastic materials instead of wood and canvas, a modern wind turbine can be very efficient (Figures 75 and 76). Mills with two, three and four long, slender, high-aspect-ratio blades, have been built. Some of these have diameters of 100 metres and larger ones are likely to be tried. The larger the rotor, the more power it can yield.

There is, however, another difficulty with such very large turbines. Consider the speed at which the outermost tip of a 100-metre turbine blade moves through the air. Each time the rotor turns, the tip travels:

$$2 \times 3.142 \times 50 \text{ m} = 314.2 \text{ m}$$

If the rotor were allowed to turn at the rate of 30 times per minute (quite a slow rotation), the tip would travel at a speed of 30 × 314.2 = 9426 m/minute, which is 565.56 km/h. The speed of the tip relative to the airflow would be greater, because of the relationship of the wind speed to the whole mill. The loads on a rotor turning at this speed would be high, and very strong materials would be required to prevent the vane from breaking.

Suppose the same 100-metre turbine were allowed to run at a speed of 65 r.p.m. The speed of the outer tips would be:

$$65 \times 314.2 = 20423 \text{ m/min}$$
$$= 1225.38 \text{ km/h}$$

The tips of such a rotor would be moving through the air at a speed greater than that of sound. (The speed of sound under standard conditions of temperature and at sea level air density is 1225.08 km/h). Even if the rotor was built strongly enough to withstand such tip speeds, the mill would produce sonic 'booms' from the tips — a constant series of bangs sounding like gunfire, 130 bangs per minute (assuming the rotor had two blades. A

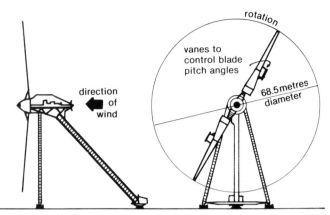

direction of wind

vanes to control blade pitch angles

rotation

68.5 metres diameter

Folland Aircraft Company design

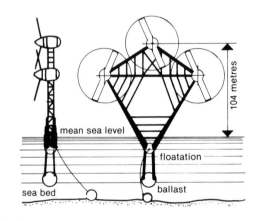

mean sea level

floatation

sea bed

ballast

104 metres

designed by Professor Heronemus

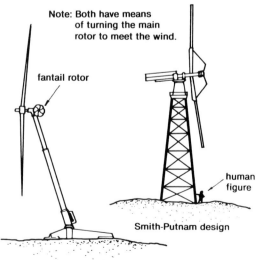

Note: Both have means of turning the main rotor to meet the wind.

fantail rotor

human figure

Smith-Putnam design

Professor Huetter's design

75. Modern designs for windmills. One of these is intended to float at sea.

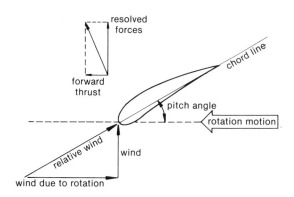

76. A modern windmill has blades shaped like a helicopter rotor in section.

rotor with three or four blades would be noisier.) Such supersonic windmills would be impractical. The *shock waves* would eventually damage the structure of the mill tower itself and there would be widespread damage to other buildings nearby, quite apart from the bad effects on people living within earshot of the mill. Mills of large diameter must always be controlled to lower speeds.

77   Wind-driven generators of the type shown here are manufactured in Australia and sold overseas. (Dunlite)

The sailing windmill

A windmill may be used to power a ship in this way. If a turbine rotor is mounted on the vessel, with a driving belt or gears to the shaft of a water propellor, the aerial rotor will turn the waterscrew, providing the mill is facing the relative wind. Since water is a denser medium than air, the windmill rotor has to be large but the water screw can be quite small. The mill can be trimmed round to face the relative wind, very much in the same way as a land mill is turned to face the natural breeze. An interesting point about such a windmill-driven boat is that it can sail directly into the wind, which no ordinary sailing ship can ever do. When running into wind, the speed of the boat increases the speed of the relative wind across the decks, so the windmill gains power. When sailing downwind, the situation is reversed; as the boat speeds up, the strength of the relative wind declines and the power from the windmill becomes less until, when the boat is moving at the same speed as the wind, the mill does not turn at all.

Things to do:

1   Make a model of a simple paddlewheel wind turbine. Try it in air flows of different strengths.

2   Make a model Savonius rotor from two half aluminium cans and plywood discs, as shown in Figure 78. The cans may be tried in different positions to find the most effective way of arranging them. With help from someone who can operate steel cutting and welding apparatus, it is not very difficult to make a larger rotor which can generate enough current to charge a car battery and so work a small electric lamp. If old oil drums are to be used, make sure they are cleaned inside and out and free from flammable gases, before cutting or welding.

3   Make a blade-type wind turbine from sheet metal, and try the effect of different blade pitch angles by twisting them.

4   Model shops will supply simple plastic or wooden airscrews (propellers) intended for model aeroplanes of various types.

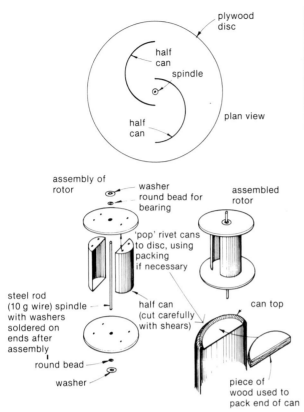

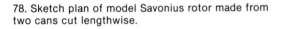

78. Sketch plan of model Savonius rotor made from two cans cut lengthwise.

79   The Darrius rotor, shown here under test at an experimental site, is sometimes more efficient than the simpler Savonius type of rotor. The bow-shaped aerofoils are flexible, which aids control of the speed of rotation. (Author)

Obtain such a propeller and study it carefully. Note the way the pitch angle changes along the blade, and the shape of the blades, especially in cross section. Try the propeller as a windmill rotor. Turn it round on the spindle to see if it works better one way round than the other.

Things to find out:

1   Are there any windmills working in your district? If so, what are they used for?

2   Find out if any plans exist for making greater use of windmills for power generation in your area.

chapter 6

spinning

Boomerangs

The Aboriginal people of Australia are believed to have developed the returning boomerang at least 10 000 years ago. Outside Australia, various different types of throwing sticks have been used by hunters at different periods. Some of these weapons resembled boomerangs in some ways. In ancient Egypt, curved sticks, looking very like boomerangs, have been found in tombs dating back to 2300 B.C. but models of these have not proved capable of returning to the thrower. They were probably 'non-returning' boomerangs, weapons which would spin in the air and which would fly further than an ordinary spear or throwing club. Curved clubs which may sometimes have been thrown have been

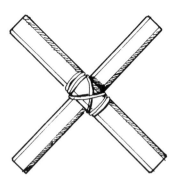

81. A simple cross boomerang made from two rulers bound together.

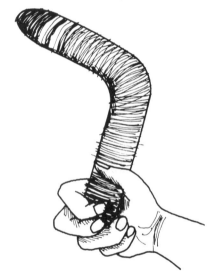

grip for a right-handed thrower

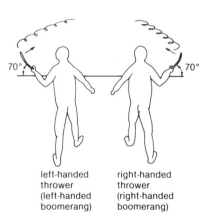

70°   70°

left-handed   right-handed
thrower   thrower
(left-handed   (right-handed
boomerang)   boomerang)

view from behind the throwers

80. How to throw boomerangs.

found in prehistoric sites in Europe, India, Africa and the Americas. Their shape and spinning flight probably enabled the user to strike targets at a greater range than was possible with an ordinary stick, but none of these has proved to be a true returning boomerang of the Australian type.

The discovery was certainly not made all at once. Probably it was noticed that throwing clubs which had a flattish cross-section, rather than round, would sometimes fly further than expected and, when thrown with a spin, might even soar upwards before falling. Over many years, this early type of boomerang was improved and developed. When the first European settlers arrived, the boomerang was in use almost everywhere throughout Australia, both as a hunting and war weapon and as a plaything. Examples were sent to Europe and America and boomerang throwing became quite popular as a hobby and sport. Now there are boomerang clubs and societies in many countries and world championships are held regularly.

It is easy to make a returning boomerang from wood or plastic material. With a small amount of practice anyone can learn to throw it in such a way that it returns towards the thrower, although to make it land very close every time requires much skill (Figure 80).

It is not necessary for the boomerang to have only two arms. Quite a good one may be made by binding together two ordinary wooden rulers, flat side down, to make a simple cross (Figure 81). Six- or even eight-armed boomerangs may be made in the same way, but the curved two-arm type is very effective (Figure 82).

When thrown, the boomerang must be

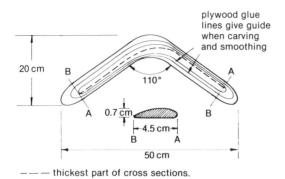

— — — thickest part of cross sections.

Right-handed boomerang, thickness distribution and cross-section. A = leading edge, B = trailing edge of arm. A left-handed boomerang should be a mirror image of this form. Perfect accuracy is not necessary.

82. A boomerang carved from thick plywood.

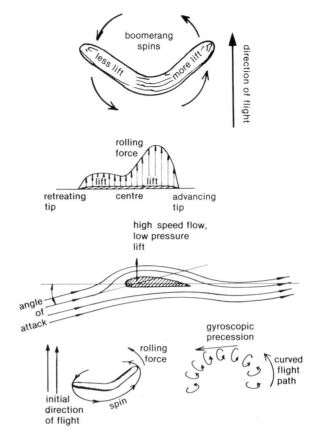

Bernoulli's theorem operates. The airflow over the cross-section of the boomerang creates a difference in pressure which produces a lift force.
The greater speed of the advancing arm of the boomerang creates more lift on that side, so tending to roll the boomerang over.
Gyroscopic precession turns this into a circular flight path.

83. How a boomerang flies.

made to spin rapidly, somewhat like a windmill rotor, so each arm of the boomerang behaves like a windmill blade. The cross section of the blade is cambered, so that as it moves through the air, Bernoulli's theorem operates; a pressure difference is created. This enables the boomerang to fly (Figure 83). As the spinning flight goes on, on one side the speed of rotation is combined with the speed of forward movement. The blade on this side is moving very rapidly through the air. The speed of the rotation is added to the speed of the whole boomerang. The other blade is moving much more slowly relative to the air; the forward motion of the whole boomerang reduces the speed of airflow over the blade itself. The lift provided by the two blades is unequal, and this tends to tip the boomerang upside down. The spin, however, causes the whole boomerang to behave like a gyroscopic wheel. As the unequal lift on the arms tries to twist the boomerang over, the gyroscopic force acts to turn it round to one side. The toppling tendency is thus changed into a turning flight and the boomerang follows a curved path, spinning all the time as it goes.

The knack of throwing with a spin is soon picked up with a little practice. Different sizes and shapes of boomerang follow different flight paths. The angle and direction of the initial launch must be judged correctly to achieve a return flight. The direction of the throw in relation to the wind also makes a great difference. Other important factors are the cross section of the blades, which may be changed by carving the wood or even by twisting the whole arm, and the mass

distribution. The mass distribution may be altered by attaching moveable lead weights to the arms. If the weights are moved in towards the centre of the boomerang, so that the mass is concentrated near the middle, the flight path tends to follow a smaller circle than when the weights are moved outwards, concentrating the mass towards the tips.

The full explanation of boomerang flight is quite complicated and requires knowledge of physics and mathematics. Some interesting experiments have been done, by Felix Hess, with boomerangs fitted with small lights. At night the flight path may be photographed by cameras mounted with shutters fixed open. The resulting trace may then be compared with theoretical paths plotted with the aid of a computer (Figure 84).

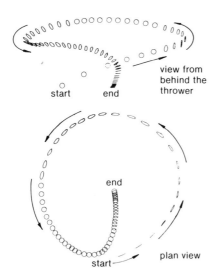

The small circles represent the boomerang's position at intervals of 1/10 second.

84. An example of a boomerang's calculated flight path plotted by a computer. (Felix Hess, *Boomerangs, Aerodynamics and Motion*)

The Australian Aborigines showed, of course, that such advanced studies were not necessary for someone to learn how to make and use boomerangs.

Things to do:

1   Make some simple boomerangs following the drawings given. Note that left- and right-handed throwers should shape the blades differently. Practice throwing the boomerangs on a suitable, clear open space such as a school sports ground. Boomerangs can be dangerous, so make sure no one is likely to be struck, and watch out for the successful throw which returns to hit the thrower or those standing nearby. Try the effect of adding small weights to the tips of the boomerang.

2   Take the front wheel from a bicycle, and hold it firmly by the ends of the axle while someone else sets the wheel spinning as rapidly as possible. Try to change the direction of the axle to a new position while the wheel is still spinning. Note the direction and strength of the gyroscopic forces felt. Similar forces, together with the unequal aerodynamic lift of the spinning arms, are responsible for the boomerang's curved flight. This experiment also helps to explain how it is possible to ride a bicycle 'hands off'.

Things to find out:

1   In some early military aeroplanes, such as the Sopwith Camel, the whole of the engine rotated, the propeller being bolted securely to the body of the motor itself. Such a massive rotary engine acted as a powerful gyroscope at the front of the aircraft. Try to work out what effects this had on such aeroplanes when they made sharp turns in aerial combat.

2   Where and when are the world championships for boomerang throwing held? Who is the current champion?

Spinning cricket balls and baseballs

Some cricket bowlers and baseball pitchers can make the ball swerve in the air. This is not at all the same thing as the ball turning as it bounces on the pitch, nor is it merely an effect of the wind, although the best bowlers do also make use of whatever wind may be blowing, to move the ball and so, they hope, deceive the batsman.

The ball can be made to swing in the air even if there is no wind. It is done by spinning the ball as fast as possible, while at the same time directing it at the stumps. The same effect is sometimes seen with table tennis balls if they are spinning rapidly; golfers, too, find their shots going astray if they have not allowed for the spin. The cause of the mid-air turn is a pressure difference caused by the Bernoulli effect.

If a ball moves through the air with no spin, the air flow simply divides and passes over it, the pattern being the same on both sides. Behind the ball there is usually a region of separated flow, which causes drag and tends to slow the ball down. As the flow passes over the ball, there is a reduction of air pressure all round, but the reduction is equal in all directions so the ball does not curve to one side or the other.

The pattern of air flow round a spinning ball is different (Figure 85). As the ball flies through the air spinning, friction on one side tends to speed the airflow up while on the other side it is slowed down. On the side where the flow is faster, the air pressure is reduced more than on the slower side. There is a difference between the two which moves the ball sideways. The faster the spin, the greater this effect. Unfortunately from the bowler's point of view, the air drag tends to

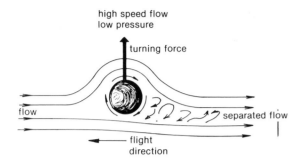

The Bernoulli effect causes the ball to swerve in flight.

85. The airflow over a spinning cricket ball.

slow the rate of spin down quite quickly, so the initial rotation given by the wrist, hand and fingers just at the moment of releasing the ball has to be very powerful if the effect is to last long enough to puzzle the batsman. It is very difficult to give the ball such a spin and at the same time direct it accurately down the wicket. The spin also causes the ball to change direction as it touches the ground, so to play against a good spin bowler is extremely difficult for the batsman.

The surface of the ball makes a great deal of difference. A fast bowler prefers a new, polished cricket ball, because the air drag is less if the surface is smooth and shiny. An older ball, which has lost its shine, will be slowed down in flight by the extra drag, but if spinning it may turn in the air better than the new ball. The extra drag caused by the dull surface helps to create the Bernoulli effect and the mid air swerve. The condition of the seam where the cover of the ball is joined also affects the flight and the way the ball pitches.

Since a spinning ball can generate an aero-dynamic reaction force, it is not very surprising to find that a turning cylinder will do the same thing. It was realised in the early days of aviation that a lifting force could be obtained from a long horizontal spinning cylinder. It was suggested that an aeroplane should be built with the wings replaced by such a lifting device, the engines being used to spin the cylinder as well as propellers to drive the air-craft forwards. No such aircraft was built, but it was shown that a ship could be driven by a series of tall spinning cylinders getting the driving force from the air instead of relying on a water screw or sail (Figure 86). Such a ship had no advantage over the ordinary, screw-driven vessel, so the invention was never taken any further. In recent times, new

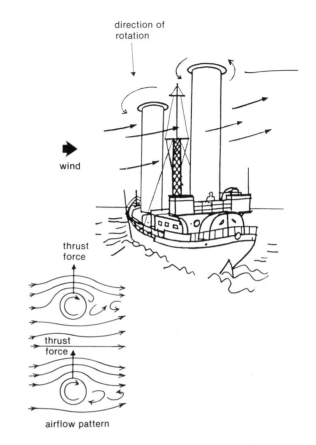

86. The rotor powered ship.

forms of airship have been proposed, using this principle. The helium in the spherical or cylindrical gas bag will provide most of the lift, but if the whole gasbag rotates around a horizontal axis, additional aerodynamic lift will result.

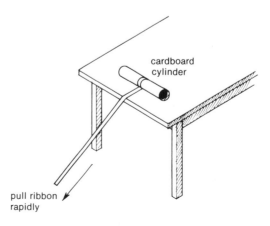

87. An experiment to show the lifting effect of a spinning cylinder.

Things to do:

1   With a table tennis bat and ball, try to make the ball swerve in the air by giving it a strong spin. A good table tennis player can demonstrate this, and a player who does not know how to do it will become better if this trick is developed and practised.

2   Wrap a ribbon around a cardboard tube, and use it to spin the tube rapidly off a table, as shown in Figure 87. The tube will move forwards, spinning rapidly. The spin will cause it to lift itself upwards for a short flight.

3   Practise spin bowling. Not many people can bowl accurately, at a good pace, and also turn the ball in the air, but it can be done. Baseball pitchers who can achieve the aerial swerve also have an advantage.

Things to find out:

1   How fast does a cricket ball travel when bowled by a fast bowler? What about the speeds of balls in other sports? In which ball game does the ball travel the fastest?

2   What regulations govern the size and type of balls used in different games?

chapter 7

kites

Like sailing ships, kites have been used for a very long time indeed and it is not sure who invented them. Some of the earliest records tell of kite flying in China several centuries before the Christian era in the West, but it has been claimed that kites were known even earlier among the seafaring people of the Pacific Islands and what is now Malaysia. Quite likely it was experience with sails and ropes that gave people the idea that a sail could rise into the air bodily.

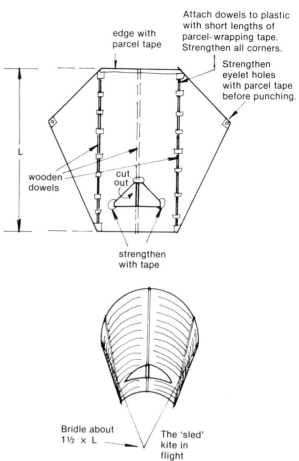

edge with parcel tape

Attach dowels to plastic with short lengths of parcel-wrapping tape. Strengthen all corners.

Strengthen eyelet holes with parcel tape before punching.

wooden dowels

cut out

strengthen with tape

Bridle about 1½ × L

The 'sled' kite in flight

Copy the shape fairly closely. The size is not very important. Plastic sheet from a garbage bag may be used.

89. The design of a simple 'sled' kite made from plastic sheeting and two or three light wooden spines.

88   Professor Hiroi, a well-known Japanese kite expert, with Lisa Carson, who has made a small but effective kite from a garbage bag. The long streamer stabilises the kite.

The simplest form of kite is just a sail-like piece of cloth with strings at the corners, and sticks or light spars to hold the edges apart. Plastic sheeting which allows no air to escape through the pores, as cloth does, is often used now (Figure 89).

The aerodynamic reaction on a kite is just the same as that on a sail, but instead of the force being directed horizontally to drive a ship, the kite is turned so that there is a lifting effect (Figure 90).

The line, or, with large kites, strong rope or steel cable, is formed into a bridle which holds the sail at an angle of attack to the airflow. There is a pressure difference between the upper and the lower sides, owing to the Bernoulli effect. The Square Law applies as usual. Doubling of the wind speed increases the aerodynamic forces by four times. The reaction may be resolved in two directions, the upward component of the force being called the *lift* and the horizontal component is the *drag*. For the kite to fly steadily the bridle must be adjusted so that the angle of attack, or trim, is correct. In different wind strengths, the bridle may need various adjustments for the best results.

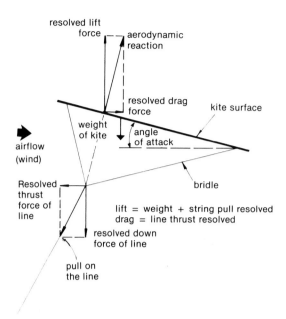

Note: For steady flight in equilibrium, the lift force must equal the weight plus the downforce on the bridle; the thrust force must equal the drag.

90. The forces acting on a simple kite.

The force in the kite line may be resolved, just as the aerodynamic reaction may. The forward pulling component may be called the *thrust*; it prevents the kite drifting away with the wind. The downward component is part of the load carried by the kite. This is added to the weight force caused by gravity acting on the mass of the kite, directly downwards. If a kite is made to carry some heavy object, the weight of this also becomes part of the load. When a kite is flying steadily in

equilibrium, all the resolved forces balance one another. The thrust equals the drag, the lift equals the total of weight and load forces.

As with sails, the position of the centre of pressure on the kite is very important (Figure 91). For instance, if the kite is tail heavy, it will tend to rear up and stall (the airflow will separate). The kite will fly steadily only when the weight, line and any other forces all balance at the aerodynamic centre of pressure.

In gusty weather, or if the line is jerked, equilibrium is upset and the kite will move to and fro. Fighting kites may be steered by clever timing of a pull on the line when a wind gust has turned the kite to one side or the other. The idea in kite fighting is to cut the line belonging to another kite. A short section of the line is roughened, with sharp sand or glass powder and glue, to act as a cutter. To win a kite fight against an expert is very difficult.

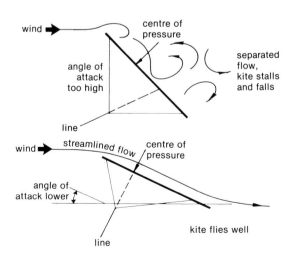

91. The importance of the centre of pressure.

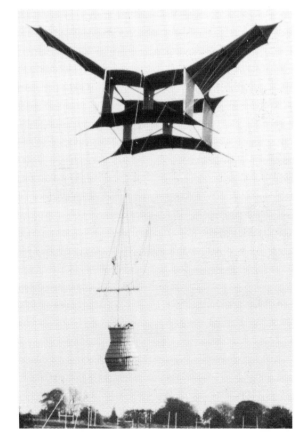

92 A modern version of the Cody man-lifting kite. The basic design is that of a Hargrave box kite with large stabilising wings added. The passenger rides in the basket suspended from pulleys running on the line. (R. G. Moulton)

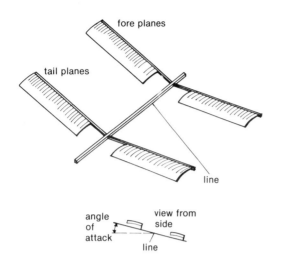

93. A tandem kite of the type flown by Lawrence Hargrave.

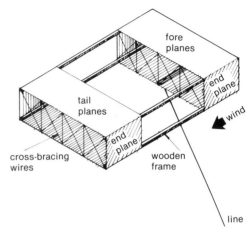

94. A box kite of Hargrave type.

Lawrence Hargrave

For most purposes, it is very important that the kite should not jerk or swing wildly about as the fighting kite does. The kite should be stable. That is, if it is disturbed by a gust, it should steady itself and return quickly to its correct flying attitude. Unstable kites often turn right over and crash to the ground without warning. For stability, kites are often fitted with tail streamers. The drag of the streamer is intended to keep pulling the head of the kite into the wind.

Better ways of stabilising a kite were discovered in Australia by Lawrence Hargrave who lived at Stanwell Park near Sydney from his arrival there in 1866 till his death in 1915. His kite designs became well known to the pioneer aviators in other parts of the world. One of Hargrave's early kites had two pairs of wings in a tandem arrangement (Figure 93). Viewed from the front, the surfaces were tilted upwards at an angle, called the *dihedral* angle. This gave the kite stability in the lateral or sideways direction. If a gust of wind tipped the kite sideways, the dihedral caused the wings on the high side to lose lift while the surfaces on the down side

lifted more strongly, tending to set the kite upright again. The rear or tailplane gave this type of kite stability in pitch. The tail acted rather like the fletching on an arrow, keeping the front wing always at the best angle of attack and pointing into the wind. Hargrave discovered that once this kite was properly set up, it needed no bridle. The line could be attached quite simply at one point close to the centre of pressure, and it would fly perfectly. Hargrave's tandem kite would have flown without a line, as a simple glider. He did build a very large version of it to carry a man, but it was wrecked by a gust of wind before leaving the ground. Probably the structure was too flimsy for such a large aircraft. Modern gliders and sailplanes, both model and full-sized, are often launched just like this early kite. When the towline is released by the pilot, they fly stably. It is not necessary to make the tailplane so large, but Hargrave had discovered principles of stability which are still used in aeroplanes and gliders.

Hargrave went on to develop the box kite, which could be made very light and strong, yet with a very large area of lifting surface (Figure 94). By attaching several of these large box kites together in a train, he lifted himself into the air at Stanwell Park, on 12 November 1894, and descended safely (Photo 92). This was not the first time a kite was used to lift a human being. George Pocock in England made a kite to lift his daughter, Martha, to a height of 100 metres in 1825. She descended safely. Pocock also made a large kite to pull a carriage and used this for a road journey in 1827.

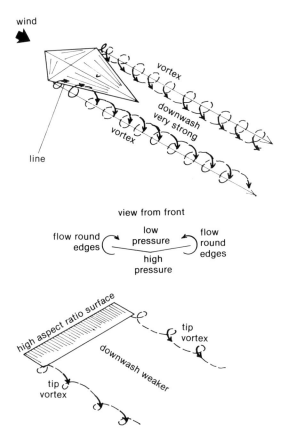

view from front

95. Vortex flows caused by air spilling from high pressure side of lifting surface to low pressure side.

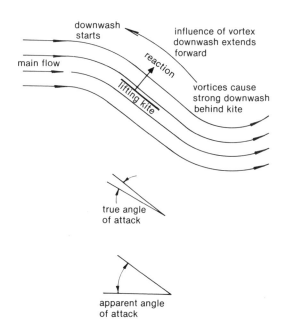

96. The effect of vortex-induced downwash on the flow around a simple lifting surface of low aspect ratio.

Downwash and vortices

Most simple kites have lifting surfaces at least as long from nose to tail as they are across. The common diamond shaped kite is longer than its breadth or span from side to side. The *planform*, especially the aspect ratio (the ratio of the fore-to-aft average width or chord, to the crosswise span), makes a very great difference to the way a particular kite flies.

If the airflow over an ordinary kite could be made visible, it would look like that in the diagram (Figure 95). The air on the under side, which is at higher pressure than that above, spills round the outer edges of the lifting surface, just as the air spills round the upper and lower edges of a sail on a ship. This spilling of air creates strong rotating vortices which trail off behind the kite. The vortices waste a lot of energy and increase the drag of the kite.

The trailing vortices affect the flow pattern all round the kite, not only around the edges. Since air behaves like a fluid, a change in one part of the flow pattern tends to distort the flow in other areas too. This is probably easier to understand with visible fluid flows in water. If a flat stick is moved through the fluid, vortices may be seen trailing off behind, forming small whirlpools. Ahead of the moving stick, the flow also changes as the fluid begins to move some distance ahead of the approaching object. In the same way the air flow ahead of a lifting kite begins to feel the effects of the trailing vortices before they arrive. There is a strong down-turning or *downwash* of the flow both in front of and behind the kite. The result is that the angle at which the air actually approaches the kite is much less than it seems to be from the ground.

Kites of low aspect ratio often fly at angles of 45 degrees or so to the horizontal. The air, because of the downwash in front, actually flows over them at something much less, perhaps only fifteen or twenty degrees. The true angle of attack to the airflow is very much less than it appears. If this were not so, such kites would not fly at all. If the air really came at an angle of 45 degrees to the kite, the flow would separate or stall, and very little lifting force would be created. The kite would not be capable of supporting itself. The downwash caused by the strong trailing vortices induces a change of angle of attack and prevents the stall (Figure 96).

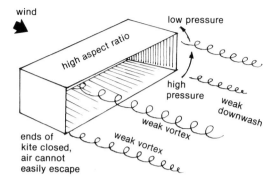

97. How the box kite reduces the tip vortices and decreases downwash effects.

Hargrave's box kites

Hargrave's box kites were somewhat different. The lifting surfaces were much greater in span, from side to side, than from back to front. The aspect ratio (span to average chord) was higher. At the tips of the wings, Hargrave continued the fabric covering to close in the ends of the double wing or biplane, box-like, framework (Figure 97). The air did not spill so easily from the high pressure side to the low pressure side of the wing, so the whirling vortices were much less strong. These kites thus caused less drag, and there was much less downwash both behind and in front. They generated more lift at low angles of attack. The angle of the bridle had to be changed to reduce the angle of trim. When this was done, the kites lifted very strongly and were capable of carrying heavy loads. Hargrave's tandem kite also had wings of high aspect ratio.

Kites have been used in many different ways. In some countries it is a custom to fly kites on certain holy days of the year, and send prayers up the line to the sky. The prayer is written on a piece of paper which hangs on a small ring on the line and is pushed up by the wind. It is also said that in ancient China, kites were sometimes used to carry bombs over enemy cities during a siege. In more recent times, especially since the invention of the powerful box kite, they have been used to carry meteorological instruments, aerial cameras, radio aerials and even people. A new idea in Australia is to use huge kites to generate electric power. These kites would fly at great altitudes to reach the very strong jetstream winds that blow almost constantly in the stratosphere. They would carry wind driven generators and send the current down the kite line to earth.

This interesting combination of windmill and kite is, so far, only a theoretical possibility, but it may one day prove useful (see also Figure 184).

Things to do:

1   Make some kites following the patterns given in a book of kite designs, and fly them. Experiment with different shapes and different bridles. **Do not fly kites anywhere near overhead electric power lines**. Learn how to make a fighting kite and how to control it in the air. Organise a kite fighting competition. Some modern kites have two lines and can perform various aerobatics. If possible, make or borrow such a kite and learn how to steer it. How does the steering system work?

2   When you have a simple kite flying steadily, try sending messages up the line. Parachutes and small model gliders may be launched in the same way. Books on kites will be able to show you how this is done.

3   One kite may help to lift another, if they are joined in train as shown in Photo 98. Try this.

Note: Kites must not be flown near aerodromes nor above legal height limits in other areas.

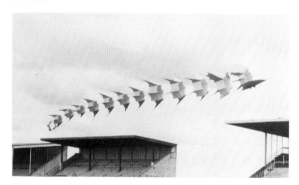

98   A train of steerable kites in the form of a serpent. To get such a complex kite into the air and control it safely is a task for experts. (R. G. Moulton)

Things to find out:

1   Find out about Benjamin Franklin's kite-flying experiments, but do not attempt to repeat them: your research should soon give you the reason why his trials were very dangerous.

2   Find out if there is a kite flying club or association in your region. You may even form your own, if sufficient people are interested.

chapter 8

parachutes

The idea of the parachute, like the kite, began with the ordinary sail. It was realised that if a sail could drive a ship and lift a person into the air, it might save one from falling. One of the first designs for a parachute, sketched by Fausto Veranzio in 1595, was a square sail held open by four light wooden spars with a rope harness.

There was no real use for such devices until the balloon made human flight possible. The first successful parachute jump took place in 1797 in Paris when Jacques Garnerin dropped from his balloon at a height of about 1000 metres using a parachute with a light framework covered with fabric and opening like a very large umbrella. He landed safely but his parachute swayed to and fro wildly as it came down (Figure 99).

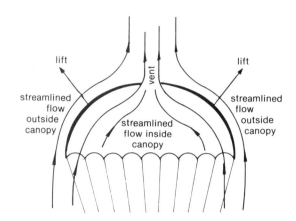

100. With a central vent the flow remains streamlined and the parachute descends safely.

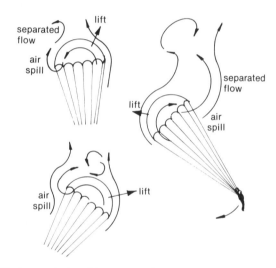

99. A parachute with no central vent swings dangerously from side to side as air spills out from the canopy and vortexes form.

It was later realised that a parachute would be unstable unless it had a vent at the top to allow some of the air to escape by flowing smoothly instead of spilling irregularly around the sides of the canopy (Figure 100). Garnerin made many more safe jumps and parachuting became a popular feature at balloon demonstrations and shows during the nineteenth century. When the aeroplane came into use, parachutes were developed without any poles or framework. These could be folded up into fairly small packs and strapped to the aviator's body. They were not very reliable at first. Many different sorts and weaves of cloth were tried, including linen, cotton and silk. The closeness of the weave and the ability of the cloth to stand the shock

of opening without ripping were vitally important. A canopy that had become damp or which had been packed carelessly might fail to open. Nowadays, artificial fabrics are used and a properly packed parachute is very reliable. One of the most important improvements was the addition of a 'pilot chute', a small parachute which jumps out and springs open immediately as soon as the pack is opened (Figure 103). The pilot chute pulls the main canopy out into the airflow.

Many pilots have been saved by parachutes of this type. In the World War II, troops were dropped into battle by parachute and were often supplied by air, using large parachutes to land heavy equipment, guns, road vehicles and ammunition. Since then military parachutists have formed a part of most armies. Secret agents and saboteurs have also been dropped, at night, behind enemy lines.

Parachutes, often of the ribbon type which open with less of a shock, are also used as airbrakes on some jet aircraft and gliders, and they are used to bring space capsules gently to earth after re-entering the atmosphere.

The ordinary parachute canopy used for emergencies, when opened, forms a simple umbrella shape and is designed only to save life. It can be steered only to a very small extent. The landing can be quite hard and untrained people can easily be injured on touch-down or by being dragged across the ground by the wind. The sport parachutist uses a parachute which can be steered. Segments of the umbrella-shaped canopy are left open (Figure 102). The air spills out of

101 Ribbon parachutes are sometimes used as airbrakes for landing in modern sailplanes. Without brakes, such a refined aircraft needs a very much larger landing area. Note that this Swiss-registered 'Libelle' sailplane also has airbrakes in the wing, and that they are partly open. To save drag, the wheel is retracted in normal flight. (Theo Heimgartner)

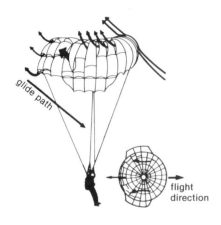

By careful positioning of vents, the flow in and over a parachute canopy allows it to glide forward. It may be steered by the jumper to land at a chosen spot.

102. Steering a parachute.

these open sections, and there is more aerodynamic reaction on one side of the canopy than the other. This drives the parachute along in one direction, and by pulling on the harness the parachutist can turn to either side and move in the direction required to land at a target.

Some of the most advanced parachutes come close to being true gliders. In these the canopy is best thought of as a sort of wing.

The lift is provided by the Bernoulli effect as the air flows smoothly over the curved fabric, with a difference of pressures above and below.

Skydiving

A free-falling parachutist or skydiver also uses aerodynamic reaction forces to control his fall. By taking up a position with arms and legs stretched out and the body arched backwards, the maximum air drag is created and the speed of fall is reduced to its slowest (Figure 103). This falling position is also stable. The outstretched arms and legs then may be used as controls. Moving the arms into a back-swept position and arching the body slightly forward pitches the parachutist into a head-down position and increases the speed. It is possible to track forwards through the air while still falling (Figure 104). Moving the arms and legs in other ways allows turns and acrobatics to be performed, and skydivers may steer to link up with one another, perform aerial formation flights and so on.

Of course the parachute canopy must be opened in good time for a safe landing and a reserve is always carried in case the first parachute fails for any reason.

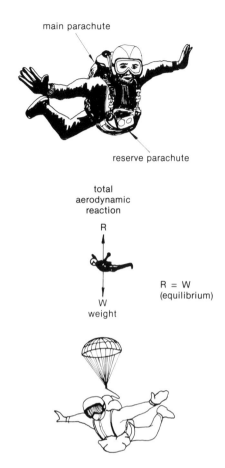

main parachute

reserve parachute

total
aerodynamic
reaction

R

R = W
(equilibrium)

W
weight

On pulling the ripcord, the pilot parachute springs out and pulls the main canopy from its pack.

103. The 'stable spread' position used by sky divers.

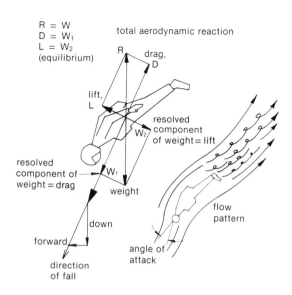

$R = W$
$D = W_1$
$L = W_2$
(equilibrium)

total aerodynamic reaction

R

drag,
D

lift,
L

resolved
component
of weight = lift

W_2

resolved
component of
weight = drag

W_1

weight

down

forward

angle of
attack

flow
pattern

direction
of fall

104. The fast-fall and forward-tracking position used by sky divers.

2   Arrange for a parachutist to show how a parachute is made and how it is re-packed after use. A school gymnasium or hall will provide enough space for such a demonstration, but ensure the floor is clean first. At most air shows, skydiving will be demonstrated and much can be learned by watching these events carefully. Do not attempt any kind of parachuting or skydiving without proper training and well-proved equipment.

Things to do:

1   Make some simple model parachutes and fly them. They may be dropped from a tall building or carried up by a kite, balloon or model aeroplane. Try different shapes of canopy and different materials. Try varying the mass of the load.

Things to find out:

1   Apart from skydiving and emergency rescues, what other uses are made of parachutes? What records are recognised for parachutists? How are parachuting competitions scored?

2   Find out how parachutists are trained.

chapter 9

gliders

Although there are many myths and stories about people flying or trying to fly by making wings like those of a bird and leaping from towers or cliffs, it was only when people began to think carefully and scientifically about flight that any real progress was made. Balloons came first, but they could only drift along in whatever direction the wind took them. Driving them through the air by oars or flappers was tried, but there were at first no light, powerful engines and human muscles were not strong enough to make much difference. Even when Giffard tried an airship with a small steam engine in 1852, there was not enough power to make headway against the wind. It was more than forty years later that the invention of the petrol engine made both the steerable or dirigible airship and the powered aeroplane possible.

Even before the balloon, enough was known about sails, kites and parachutes for a glider to be built. There were even small toy helicopters as early as 1325, which would rise into the air when made to spin. What was lacking was anyone who could bring all these separate ideas together to make a flying machine which, unlike a balloon, would be controllable and capable of going in any direction.

George Cayley

In 1799 Sir George Cayley, an Englishman, sketched the design of a simple glider, which he described as a 'governable parachute' (Figure 105). The main lifting surface, or wing, was a square sail, but he provided a tail to give stability and control.

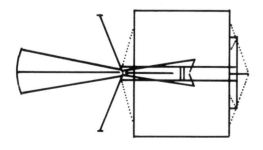

105. Sir George Cayley's sketch plan of a glider, drawn in 1799.

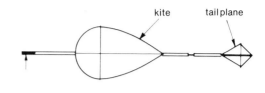

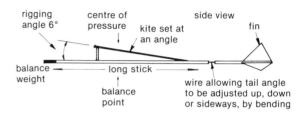

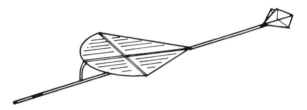

106. George Cayley's kite glider model of 1804.

A few years later he made and flew a model glider which was nothing more than a simple kite mounted on a stick at an angle, with a tail like an arrow (Figure 106). By altering the setting of the tail and adding a weight at the front of the stick to balance the glider at the centre of pressure, he was able to trim the model to fly steadily. He launched it by hand from the top of a hill and saw it glide smoothly down to land in the fields below.

It was Cayley who was able to bring together all the different sorts of knowledge and experience, from sailing, kite flying and parachuting, to make the first truly successful heavier-than-air, steerable, flying machine.

In following years he designed and built, or had built for him, other experimental models and in 1849 he tried a glider which carried a boy for a short flight. In 1853 he persuaded his coachman to fly in his largest glider (Figures 107 and 108). The wing was still just like a very large kite and the coachman was expected to control the aircraft by means of a tiller. A modern copy of this man-carrying glider has been flown.

Cayley died in 1857. There were no lightweight engines in his time, so he never tried to fit one to his gliders. Other people read about his work and learned from it. In 1891 the German Otto Lilienthal began with

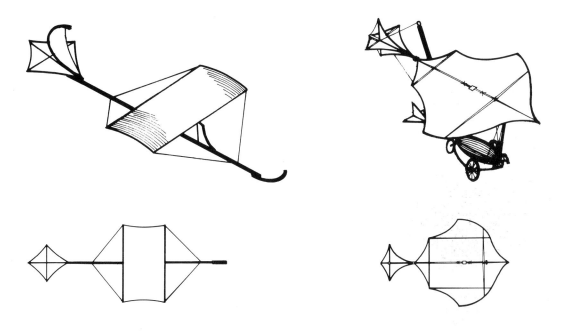

107. Cayley's model glider of 1853.

108. Cayley's man-carrying glider which flew successfully in 1853.

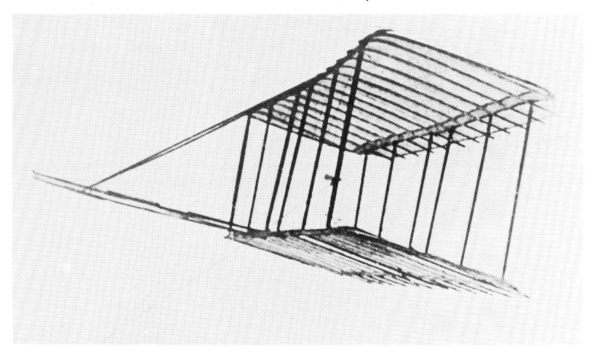

109 An early Wright Brothers kite, used in their experiments leading to controlled flight in gliders, and finally to the first powered flight.

simple hang gliders which he steered by moving his body, and he was followed by Chanute and Montgomery in America, and Pilcher in England.

The Wright brothers combined all the discoveries made by these earlier pioneers and Hargrave's box kite principles, to build several very good gliders. When they had learned to control them safely they were ready to try a powered aeroplane (Photo 109).

How a glider flies

With a glider, the forces acting are very similar to those on a kite, but the glider does not depend on the wind to keep it flying. Instead of being held in position by a line to let the wind blow over it, the glider moves forward through the air, the movement creating a relative airflow flow over the lifting surface.

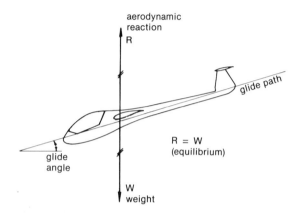

110. Forces acting on a glider in flight.

Hargrave's tandem kite, if properly balanced and trimmed, could have flown very well without a line or any wind. So long as the glider keeps moving forward with its wing at a suitable angle of attack, the airflow over the wing will obey Bernoulli's law. There will be a difference in pressure between the upper and lower sides, so an aerodynamic reaction will be created. This reaction acts against the weight force and, for steady flight, the weight and reaction must be equal (Figure 110). To

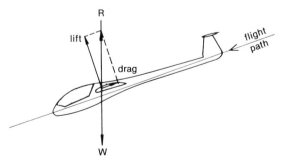

The aerodynamic reaction may be resolved into two forces: lift and drag. The lift comes almost entirely from the wing. Every part of the aircraft contributes to drag.

111. A glider's lift and drag.

start the glider moving it may be pushed forward by hand, catapulted, towed by a line like a kite, or pulled by a car or aeroplane.

Unfortunately, any movement through a fluid like air creates resistance or drag, which tends to slow the movement down and if the flow of air over the wing slows too much, the reaction will not be enough for safe flight.

Once launched, a glider has to keep itself moving and since it has no engine it cannot use any sort of artificial power to overcome the drag (Figure 111). It uses its own mass, together with gravity, to pull it forward. This is the same kind of movement as that of a car rolling down a hill, a snow skier or toboggan sliding down a slope.

The aerodynamic reaction on a glider may be resolved into two forces, the lift and the drag. The lift comes almost entirely from the wing; the drag comes from every part of the aircraft: the wing, fuselage, tail and every part which disturbs the air in any way as the glider moves through it. The weight also may be resolved into two. One part of the weight acts as a force equal and opposite to the lift. The other component of the weight acts to oppose the drag and this keeps the wing moving. Once the glider has been given its initial start these forces can all be brought into equilibrium.

To keep the glider flying, therefore, it has to be trimmed to fly at some angle, called the gliding angle, down through the air. If the glider is badly designed, it will create a lot of drag. The pilot will have to trim it to fly at a steeper angle. More of the weight force will be needed to counteract the high drag. The gliding angle will be poor (Figure 112). If the glider is very efficient, it will cause less drag and the gliding angle will be very shallow. Such an efficient glider will be able to cover a long distance from a small height.

Gliding angles are often expressed as a ratio of the distance that may be covered through the air in relation to the height lost (Figure 113). For instance, a simple hang glider of the kind a beginner might learn to fly, has a best *glide ratio* of about 6:1. That is, when well trimmed, it can fly 6 units forward through the air for every one unit of height lost. If the pilot is not flying accurately, it will not do so well.

When trimmed to fly too slowly with the wing at too high an angle of attack to the airflow, it will stall and the drag will be very great indeed. The glide ratio will then be only 2 or 3

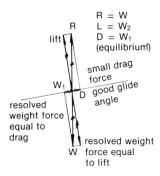

$$R = W$$
$$L = W_2$$
$$D = W_1$$
(equilibrium)

lift R

small drag force

W_1 D good glide angle

resolved weight force equal to drag

resolved weight force equal to lift

W

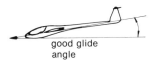

good glide angle

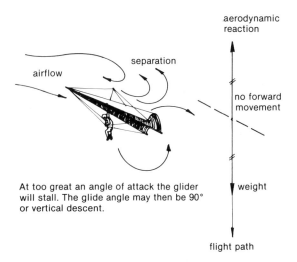

aerodynamic reaction

separation

airflow

no forward movement

weight

flight path

At too great an angle of attack the glider will stall. The glide angle may then be 90° or vertical descent.

114. Effect of a large angle of attack.

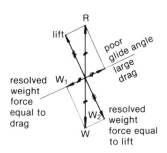

R

lift

poor glide angle

large drag

resolved weight force equal to drag W_1

W_2 resolved weight force equal to lift

W

poor glide angle

The weight force keeps the glider moving down the glide slope. If the drag is large, a steeper glide slope is required.

112. The gliding angle.

along for one down, or even 0:1, a vertical descent like a simple parachute (Figure 114). The pilot can also trim the glider to fly fast, but like a skier on a steeper hill, there will be a greater loss of height in relation to the distance covered horizontally (Figure 115).

Some modern sailplanes, used for long distance racing, have best gliding ratios of 50:1 or even better. The *sailplane* is very carefully designed so that it creates very little drag as it moves forward. The wing is made as long and narrow as possible to give it a high aspect ratio (i.e. the ratio of *span* to mean chord, as shown in Figures 63 and 116).

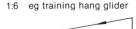

1:6   eg training hang glider

glide angle 9.46°, 6 units distance for each unit of height lost

1:40   eg standard class 15 metre sailplane

glide angle 1.43°, 40 units of distance for each unit of height lost.

113. Glide ratios.

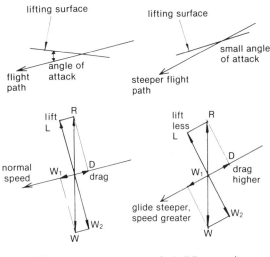

lifting surface

lifting surface

angle of attack

flight path

small angle of attack

steeper flight path

lift R
L

normal speed W_1 D drag

W_2

W

lift less R
L

W_1 D drag higher

glide steeper, speed greater W_2

W

normal gliding speed
$R = W$, $L = W_2$, $D = W_1$

fast gliding speed
$R = W$, $L = W_2$, $D = W_1$

115. Angle of attack related to gliding speed.

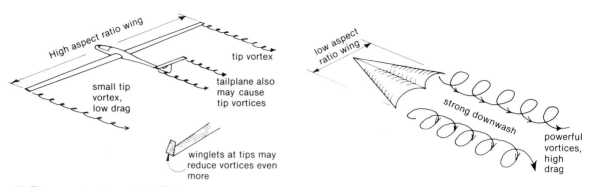

116. The aspect ratio and its effect.

117   Ferdinand Schultz, a schoolteacher, built and flew this hang-glider in 1923, flying it from the sand dunes near his home in East Prussia. (Alex Stocker)

118   The author's LS-3 sailplane, which is typical of modern racing types. The tail wheel dolly is removed before flight. Trailers similar to the one behind the LS-3 are used to bring the sailplane home by road if the pilot has to land away from base. (Author)

As mentioned in the chapter about kites, from the tips of any lifting surface there are trailing vortices which create a great deal of drag and cause downwash all round the wing. By extending the span, these vortices are reduced. Some sailplanes and aeroplanes have been fitted with winglets standing up from the tips, rather like the vertical sides of Hargrave's box kites. These are intended to stop the tip vortex.

Sailplane wing profiles

The wing is also shaped very carefully in cross section. The *wing profile* or *aerofoil* shape is designed, with the help of computers, to have very smooth airflow over as much of the surface as possible. In this way the total drag of the aerofoil is reduced as much as possible. The computer produces a perfect shape, but in practice wings cannot be built so perfectly. Most modern sailplanes are built from moulded plastics reinforced with glass fibres or carbon fibres. This method of construction enables very accurate wings to be made in the moulds. Even so, the wings get dirty and may be scratched or chipped in use. Sailplane wings should be cleaned before every flight. Even rain drops cause extra drag. In flight, the wing often becomes spattered with the bodies of small insects and if very numerous, the glide ratio worsens noticeably as the flight goes on.

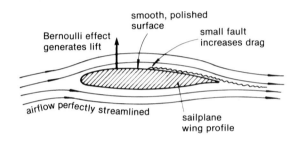

The cross-section or profile of the sailplane wing is very carefully shaped to keep the airflow smooth. Even the squashed body of an insect can disturb the air.

119. Wing profile of a sailplane.

The fuselage and tail also create drag, and everything is done to reduce this. The designer has to provide space for the pilot, in a comfortable cockpit with instruments. This ensures that the fuselage will be fairly plump, but the shape is very carefully worked out to keep the flow very smooth. Model sailplanes may have very slender 'stick' type fuselages, which cause the minimum drag.

Soaring

Flying gliders, either model or full-sized, would not be very interesting if all they could do was to glide down to the earth after launching. Lilienthal, even with his very simple hang gliders, discovered that in some conditions he could actually soar upwards, and later the Wright brothers made soaring flights of several minutes. It was realised that even though a glider has to keep itself moving by always following a downward path through the air, there are places where the air

itself rises quite rapidly. If a pilot can find such areas of rising air and keep his glider in them, *soaring* is possible. If the upcurrents are strong and enough of them can be found, a glider can stay up indefinitely. To gain height in an upcurrent, the glider is best trimmed to fly slowly with the wing at a higher angle of attack than that which gives the best glide ratio. The trim for the least rate of descent through the air is not quite the same as that which gives the best ratio of distance to height loss. Also, when the sailplane has to pass through downcurrents, which always exist when some air is going up, it is best to fly fast through them, so the pilot will trim to a high flying speed and a steeper glide ratio.

Nowadays soaring, both with models and full-sized sailplanes, is a popular sport. There are four main types of upcurrent which have proved strong enough. The simplest is created where the wind blows over a hill. The air cannot go through the hill so it must either find a route round it or rise up to flow over the top. If the hill is long and facing the wind at an angle, there will be an upcurrent all the way along and a glider may be able to use this to climb quite high and even to fly along some distance. Hill or cliff soaring by hang gliders and sailplanes (model and full-sized) is very common (Figure 120a). Soaring birds frequently use this form of lift too, enabling them to fly for hours without flapping their wings. Gulls may be seen *slope soaring* over sea walls or even above a row of houses. Other birds do the same sort of soaring over inland slopes quite often. The albatross, which flies for days on end over the ocean, soars in the upcurrents created by the wind blowing over the waves.

The second type of soaring is done in thermal upcurrents (Figure 120b). These are caused by the uneven heating of the air by the action of the sun on the ground. In any place where the ground becomes very hot, such as a patch of dark soil on a sunny day, or in a sheltered hollow, a city street, or an area of bare rocks on the face of a mountain, the air above will become heated and will tend to rise. The sailplane pilot who can find such a current will usually fly round in circles in it, so gaining altitude. The wing will be trimmed to a high angle of attack, just short of stalling, to reduce the rate of sink through the air to the minimum possible for the particular sailplane. The flight speed will be slow. When enough height has been gained by circling in the thermal, the pilot may turn

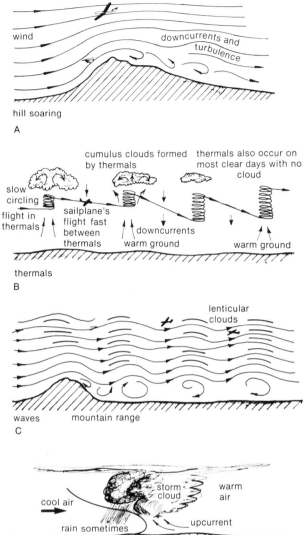

hill soaring

A

cumulus clouds formed by thermals

thermals also occur on most clear days with no cloud

slow circling flight in thermals

sailplane's flight fast between thermals

downcurrents

warm ground

warm ground

thermals

B

lenticular clouds

waves   mountain range

C

cool air

storm cloud

warm air

rain sometimes

upcurrent

fronts

D

120. Types of upcurrent used by soaring gliders and sailplanes.

have been flown across country in the same way. Generally they cannot glide so far in search of the next thermal, nor fly as fast as the sailplane, so the distances achieved are smaller.

Thermals frequently produce cumulus clouds. The air, which always contains some water vapour, cools as it rises and at some level, depending on the particular state of the atmosphere, the water will condense to form a cloud. The cumulus will grow as long as the thermal continues to bring more air and water vapour in from underneath. When the thermal dies, the cloud begins to evaporate. A sailplane pilot who arrives below a growing cloud will expect to find the thermal feeding it. It may be possible to continue the climb, on instruments, right up into the cloud to emerge from it later at a great height. If the sailplane reaches the place too late, the thermal will have died. The pilot has to try to recognise, some distance away, a cloud that is going to grow strongly, and avoid ones that will decay.

When wave upcurrents occur *wave soaring* is possible (Figure 120c). The atmosphere sometimes develops huge ripples. The *wave* may be set off by the flow over a mountain range. Riding the upward side of such a wave, occurring over the Sierra Nevada in California, a sailplane has reached the stratosphere at 45 000 ft. Smaller waves often form behind ordinary hills and there are waves which occur as ripples within the air itself even over flat ground.

Waves are frequently marked by long, whale-backed or *lenticular clouds* which stretch out for great distances more or less across the wind in lines parallel to the mountain or hill ridges setting the wave off. The air moving up the wave on the windward side reaches its condensation level and the cloud forms. As the air passes over the crest of the wave and down the other side, the water droplets evaporate again. If such a cloud is watched carefully, this motion can be seen quite clearly. Occasionally such wave clouds will form in many layers, one above the other, looking like a tall stack of plates, upside down. Where the wind blows from the highlands down across the plains, wave clouds may still be seen in parallel lines for many kilometres. Each long cloud marks the crest of a wave and each narrow gap between the lenticulars indicates a trough.

A fourth type of upcurrent forms where different air masses meet (Figure 120d). Such

away and glide at a high airspeed in search of another. If none is found, height will be lost and eventually a landing will have to be made. In good weather there are enough *thermals* to keep flying for many hours. Sailplane competitions are usually flown in thermals and the pilots are set races of several hundreds of kilometres. Distances over 1500 km have been achieved by expert pilots using this type of upcurrent. In competition flying, racing sailplanes quite often achieve average speeds of 120 km/h or more around a 300 km, 500 km or longer course. Hang gliders of the more advanced type also use thermals and frontal upcurrents are generally marked by long lines of cumulus and often cumulonimbus (thunderstorm) clouds. As the front passes through a district, the wind direction changes and there may be a period of very violent storms, with heavy rain and perhaps hail, and strong gusts. Flying gliders in such weather may be dangerous, not only because of the severe turbulence but because the aircraft may be damaged by lightning strike. A gentler type of frontal upcurrent is commonly found where a sea breeze sweeps inland as the cooler air with much water vapour tends to push under the warmer mass as it moves. A line of ragged cloud often appears at the sea breeze front and a glider pilot seeing this may use it to locate the upcurrent and ride along in it for many kilometres.

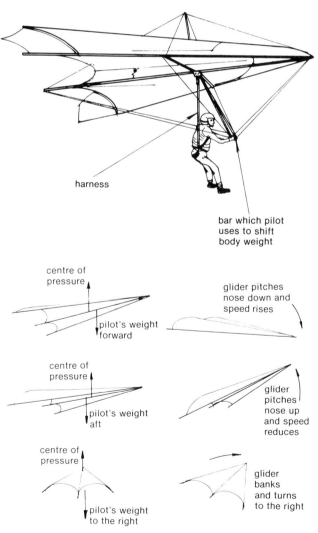

harness

bar which pilot
uses to shift
body weight

centre of
pressure

pilot's weight
forward

glider pitches
nose down and
speed rises

centre of
pressure

pilot's weight
aft

glider
pitches
nose up
and speed
reduces

centre of
pressure

pilot's weight
to the right

glider
banks
and turns
to the right

121. Controlling a hang glider.

All the different types of upcurrent which a soaring pilot may use may be discovered by studying the clouds ahead and above, or the form of the ground below. The pilot can often feel the sailplane surge up as it enters a thermal even before the instruments indicate a gain of height.

Controls

Hang gliders are usually controlled only by changing the balance (Figure 121). The pilot is suspended on a harness and holds a rigid bar which is attached firmly to the frame of the wing. By pulling on the bar the body mass is moved forward. The centre of gravity of the glider then moves ahead of the centre of pressure of the wing or sail. This causes the glider to pitch forward. By pushing on the bar the pilot shifts back and the centre of gravity moves behind the centre of pressure, causing a back or nose-up pitch. So to change the angle of attack of the wing, or to set it right again after a gust has upset it, the pilot pushes or pulls in the required direction.

To turn, or to set the glider upright after a tilting gust, a sideways pull on the bar shifts the centre of gravity to whichever side is required. For flight at low speeds, and in most conditions, this form of control is enough. In very rough air and to perform more advanced manoeuvres, hang gliders are sometimes fitted with hinged control surfaces like those of sailplanes.

The controls of a sailplane are operated from the cockpit, where the pilot sits firmly strapped into the *fuselage* (Figure 122). There is a control column or joystick which is connected by sliding rods or cables to the elevator and ailerons. The *elevator* is, usually, a simple hinged part of the tailplane. The tailplane is there to provide stability, like the tail of a kite or the fletching of an arrow. It does not add any worthwhile lift, but keeps the main wing at the required angle of attack to the airflow. By moving the elevator, the pilot can make the tailplane either lift up or push down slightly. This controls the angle of attack of the mainplane. To fly faster, the joystick is moved forward slightly, the angle of attack of the main wing is reduced and the glider flies faster. To slow down, the stick is moved back, the tail is pushed down a little, the angle of attack is increased and the sailplane slows down. The pilot can stall the aircraft by pulling back hard on the stick, or dive

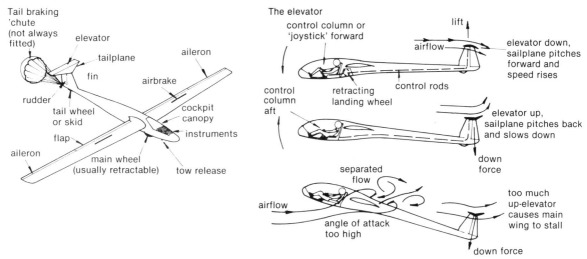

122. The controls of a sailplane.

it steeply by pushing forward. Sometimes the whole tailplane moves as an elevator.

The *ailerons* are hinged parts of the main wing. By moving the stick slightly to the right, the right hand aileron is raised and the left hand one droops. This changes the curvature or camber of the wings; the left hand one lifts more and the right hand one lifts less. The sailplane tilts over or banks to the right. Moving the stick to the left banks it to the left. When the wing is banked over, the lift force is also tilted to one side and this turns the sailplane (Figure 123). There is also a rudder which is hinged to the fin of the aircraft. This is worked by foot pedals. The action of the rudder is just like that of a boat rudder: it yaws the sailplane and is used together with the ailerons to start a turn.

On some radio-controlled model sailplanes the rudder is the only turning control. These models need the wings set at a large dihedral angle if they are to turn quickly. The rudder yaws the sailplane to one side, the dihedral banks the wing over and the lift force then produces the turn (Photo 124).

A sailplane may also have other controls such as airbrakes and wing *flaps* which change the camber of the wing all the way across the span. With their aid the pilot may manoeuvre and do most of the aerobatics that can be done by a powered aeroplane. To gain the extra energy required to loop the loop, for example, the sailplane first dives to pick up speed. Then the elevator is raised, which pushes the tail down and so increases the angle of attack of the main wing. The

extra lift created in this way pulls the sailplane up steeply and over to complete the loop. Most, but not quite all, the speed from the initial dive, is regained as the glider completes the second half of the loop, but some energy is lost and has to be made up by soaring if the pilot wants to extend the flight.

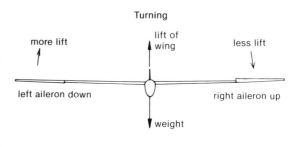

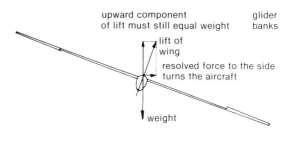

In a turn the wing must provide extra lift since a side force is required for the turn and the weight must still be balanced by an equal upward reaction. The wing angle of attack is increased slightly to achieve this.

123. The controls of a sailplane.

Things to do:

1   Make a copy of Cayley's original model glider, using a simple kite for the main wing. Try, as he had to, different weights for trimming, and different tail settings, to find the one that gives the flattest glide after a launch from a hill.

124   Sylvia Woolston prepares to launch her radio-controlled 2.54 metre-span sailplane for a contest flight. The official timekeeper stands ready with a stopwatch. (Author)

Wing

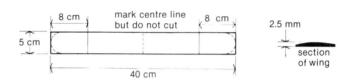

WING Cut from 2.5 to 3 mm thick balsa wood. Use a fine sanding block to shape the wing as shown. Cut off the two 8 cm-long tip sections. Sand the ends of these to fit closely at the dihedral angle shown, and glue with tips propped up 1.5 cm. Wing tips may be rounded. Balsa cement or white glue (e.g. Aquadhere) may be used for all assembly.

FUSELAGE Select a straight strip of pine, spruce, or other similar wood, 45 cm long and about 6 mm × 6 mm in section. Use a sharp wood plane to taper the rear end underneath, as shown.

Fuselage

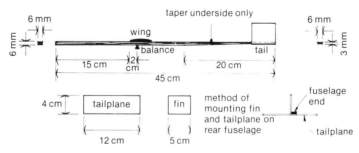

Tail

Cut tailplane and fin from 1.5 mm thick lightest possible balsa.

Assembly

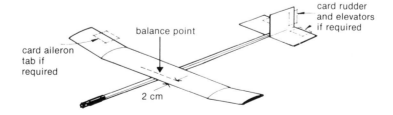

Glue wing on fuselage as shown. Check for squareness. Tailplane and fin should be in line with wing.
Balance weight three to five 50 mm round nails taped on, to balance at the point shown, for first trial flights.

125. A plan for a simple model glider.

2   Build some simple hand-launched or 'chuck' gliders from the plans given (Figure 125). A local hobby shop will be able to provide all the materials. Many different designs are possible and time, though not money, can be saved by buying a kit for a simple glider.

For the first few flights, follow the instructions on trimming given in Figure 126. If possible, get some help from an experienced model aircraft builder, to save breaking the model early in its career. After some experience has been gained, try changing the trimming weight to discover the effects of moving the centre of gravity. What happens if the centre of gravity is too far back or too far forward? Small ailerons, elevators and rudders may be made from thin card and glued on the model. By bending these slightly the effects of the controls of a glider or aeroplane may be studied.

3   Organise a duration flight contest for chuck gliders. A stopwatch will be needed. A school oval or large park without too many trees will give enough space. Some models may be broken or lost, so it is wise to build a spare one or two. Each competitor is allowed three flights, and the winner is the one with the best total time. If a model is taken up by a thermal, score only the first four minutes.

4   Arrange for someone from a local model aircraft club to demonstrate a simple towline-launched model sailplane. Plans and kits of parts for such models are not expensive and they are easy both to build and fly. Try it.

5   Follow this with a study of a radio-controlled sailplane model. With the help of an experienced person or club, learn how to control such a model and try to make thermal and slope soaring flights. Model flying clubs are always glad to have new members.

6   Get in touch with a hang gliding club and arrange for some demonstrations. Do not attempt any sort of hang gliding without joining a club and receiving proper instruction.

7   Most soaring and gliding clubs will be glad to have organised visits and will be able to arrange short passenger flights in two-seat sailplanes with an experienced pilot. A fee will be charged. Make an appointment to visit such a club and be shown a modern sailplane. Learn how sailplanes are built and inspected before flight. Parental permission will be necessary if flying is to be done by anyone under the legal age.

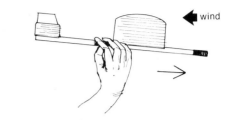

For the first flight, after checking that the model is straight and true, and balances correctly, launch the glider into wind (if any) with the nose pointing slightly down. Do not throw the model too hard to begin with. Watch the flight carefully.

If the model glides smoothly and straight to a safe landing, it is correctly trimmed.

If it climbs, stalls, then dives, swoops, climbs again, add more weight to the nose, and try again.

If it dives immediately to the ground, remove some of the nose weight.

If the model is broken, repair it. After repairs it may need further adjustments to the balance.
When correctly trimmed, more powerful launches may be attempted. Control surfaces of card may be stuck on the wing, fin and tailplane, to study their effects.

126. Trimming a model glider.

8   Look out for soaring birds. Make a note of the different species of birds which are seen slope soaring and thermal soaring. Are there any which do both?

9   Study the clouds for signs of up-currents. Note occasions when thermals produce cumulus clouds. Waves produce lenticular forms, often visible as long, smoothly shaped cloud banks aligned across the wind direction above the lee side of ranges of mountains or hills.

Things to find out:

1   Find out about the myths and legends of flying before Cayley's time.
2   What are the world and national

128   Completed, the model glider has been balanced. Depending on the length of the nose, four or five round 50 mm nails, held in place with tape, will be needed to balance the model correctly. Simple elevators of card have been glued to the tailplane, and they are bent up or down to adjust the trim. (Author)

127   Some schools run model aircraft clubs. Here students of Pembroke College, with their teacher Mrs. Wood, check the rigging of a model sailplane before covering the framework. Several identical models are built at the same time for an eventual model regatta. (Author)

records for soaring and gliding? Find out the names of the pilots who set these records and the countries where they flew.

3   Find out how gliding and soaring competitions are organised, and the names of the champion pilots.

4   Find out about the ways in which large gliders were used during World War II.

129   When they have been completed, the models are taken to the school football field for their first trial flights. (Author)

chapter 10

aeroplanes

Many people had tried to fly under power before the Wright brothers, Wilbur and Orville, made the first truly successful aeroplane. Several pioneers had managed to get a powered aeroplane off the ground and made short hops, but they could not control their machines and usually crashed immediately. One of the more successful was Richard Pearse in New Zealand. His aeroplane flew in April 1903, but crashed onto a hedge after an irregular flight of a few metres. In December of the same year the Wright biplane 'Flyer', powered by a petrol engine driving two large propellers, made the first controlled aeroplane flight.

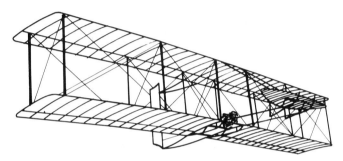

This flew under full control. The elevator was mounted in front, the rudder behind. To turn, the wings were twisted.

130. The Wright Glider of 1902.

The Wrights had realised from the start that they needed to learn how to control a flying machine in the air before trying to fly with an engine. They read everything they could find about the kite and glider flights of earlier pioneers, and built a wind tunnel to test model wings of various shapes and cross section. They flew kites, then went on to gliders (Figure 130). They discovered how to steer by twisting the wings while at the same time turning a rudder. They fitted a small, wing-like 'elevator' ahead of the main wings, which made it possible to control the angle of attack of the main wings. In these ways they solved the problems that had caused all the earlier experimenters to crash. They designed and made their own, lightweight petrol engine. At last they were ready to construct their first aeroplane, the Wright 'Flyer'.

The 'Flyer' had no wheels, so it was launched with the help of a trolley from a short length of railway track. The 'Flyer' probably would not have taken off at all without these aids and the first hop was shorter than some of their better glides. In 1904 they flew

131. The Wright Flyer of 1908.

This could stay up for two hours. Note how similar it was to the glider of 1902.

The controls of a modern aeroplane are still very much the same. (Compare figures 122 and 123)

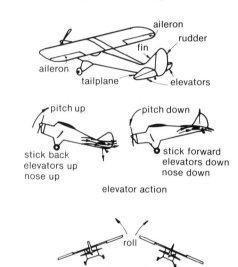

aileron action

only once for a total of five minutes. Their experiments were done almost in secret so very few people believed the newspaper stories about them. In 1905 the Wright's latest aeroplane made two flights of more than half an hour, reaching speeds of about 60 km/h. It was 1908 before they could stay up for more than an hour.

By this time several other aviators had made short flights and the general public at last realised that powered flying was possible. On the very last day of 1908 Wilbur Wright made a flight of over two hours at a meeting in France (Figure 131). They were still doing far better than anyone else.

Even when they had mastered powered flight, the Wrights still used gliders to try new inventions. One of the changes they tested in a glider in 1911 was to mount the movable elevator with the rudder behind the main wings, a layout which is still the most common.

132 The first controlled flight by an aeroplane, made in 1903 by the Wright Brothers. Two large 'pusher' propellers were mounted behind the wings of the biplane, driven by the engine which the brothers had built themselves after many gliding flights. (Smithsonian Institute)

The record breakers

After 1908 development was very rapid indeed. By 1911 aeroplanes had flown at speeds of more than 130 km/h, reached altitudes of more than 3900 m and covered 700 km non-stop in distance trials. By the end of World War I in 1918, many thousands of aeroplanes had been built. There were fast, agile fighters armed with machine guns, and bombers capable of flying long distances carrying heavy loads. After this war, it was not long before aeroplanes were being used for great flights like that by Alcock and Brown, non-stop across the Atlantic, and by Ross and Keith Smith from England to Australia. These two flights were made in Vickers Vimy twin-engined bombers which were fitted with extra fuel tanks instead of bombs.

The first commercial air lines also began with converted bombers. They were usually very uncomfortable, noisy and draughty for the passengers and expensive to operate, but they allowed people to travel across the sea at speeds far greater than the fastest ships. Over land, express railway trains were nearly as fast and much more reliable than these early aircraft, but there were many regions with no railways and bad roads. This applied to much of Australia, which was one of the first countries to develop long distance air routes.

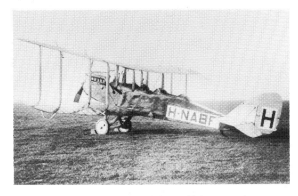

133 A De Havilland DH-9 biplane. This type of aeroplane was designed as a warplane, and many hundreds were sold cheaply after 1918. Some were used as mailplanes, and others as airliners with seats for only two or three passengers in an open cockpit.

When the aircraft factories began to produce more reliable airliners, with comfortable cabins and seating, and capable of even greater speeds, air travel became more popular.

The Fokker Trimotor, produced by the same company that had built the Fokker fighters during the war, was a successful airliner and one of this type, called 'Southern Cross', was used by the Australian Charles Kingsford Smith, with his partner Charles Ulm, for their famous long-distance flights, especially the first aerial crossing of the Pacific in 1928. It became quite fashionable for young men and women to learn to fly. At

134   The Fokker F7/3m 'Trimotor'. This was one of the first true airliners, and one known as the *Southern Cross* became famous when flown across the Pacific Ocean by Kingsford Smith. The aircraft was built mainly of wood and some steel tubing, covered with thin plywood and fabric. If one of the three engines failed, flight could continue on the other two. The undercarriage was fixed.

first they used old wartime training aeroplanes like the Avro 504 and the American Curtiss JN (the 'Jenny'). Later came such excellent types as the De Havilland Moth, in which Amy Johnson flew solo from England to Australia. Another famous pilot of this era was Bert Hinkler, a Queenslander, who, before Amy, made the first solo flight from England to Australia. Harry Hawker, another Australian, was the test pilot for the Sopwith Aircraft Company, and when the company was re-organised it took his name. The Hawker Aircraft Company later became one of the most famous. Hinkler, Hawker and Kingsford Smith were all killed in accidents. There was still much to be learned about making aeroplanes safer and navigating through bad weather.

How an aeroplane flies

A powered aeroplane flies in just the same way as a glider. The difference is that the motor keeps the wing moving forward through the air, instead of relying on gravity. The aeroplane can take off under its own power and climb to a safe height. No upcurrents are needed and as long as the motor keeps running the flight can continue indefinitely.

Early aeroplane engines frequently broke down. Fortunately, when the engine stops, an aeroplane can still glide and it is possible to make a safe descent and landing, providing there is a large enough, smooth and clear space within gliding distance. Some small aeroplanes are quite capable of soaring like a sailplane with the engine off, but they are less efficient in this than the specially designed soaring aircraft. Sailplanes sometimes have small motors enabling them to take off like an aeroplane. The engine is stopped and retracted completely when the pilot decides to begin soaring. Such self-launching gliders can be just as efficient, with the motor off, as ordinary sailplanes. Larger, faster aeroplanes cannot soar, but even they will glide some distance with the engines not working.

135   Some sailplanes are fitted with small motors, so they can take off without assistance. When the pilot wishes to begin soaring, the motor is stopped and retracts into the fuselage to reduce drag. (Eiri Avion)

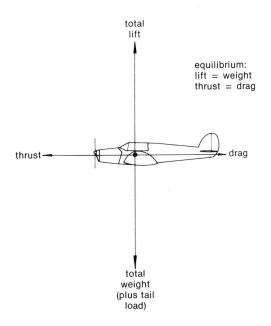

136. The forces acting on an aeroplane in level flight at steady speed.

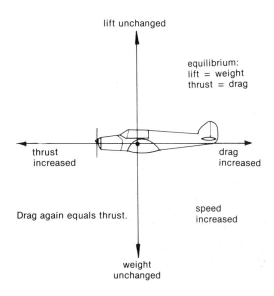

138. Flight at high speed.

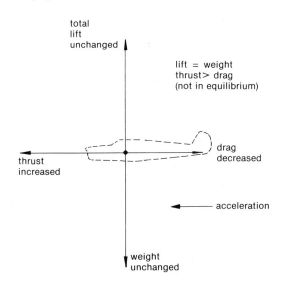

Increase of thrust or decrease of drag, or both, will allow an aeroplane to accelerate.

137. Acceleration.

When an aeroplane is in steady flight, straight and level, all the forces balance one another (Figure 136). This is a state of equilibrium. The lift generated by the wing acts vertically upwards and equals all the downward forces. The main downward force is the weight, but often there is some down-load on the tail, and the wing has to carry this too.

The engine produces thrust which acts against the drag. To make the aeroplane fly faster, either the thrust may be increased or the drag decreased, or both (Figure 137). If the pilot opens the engine up to get more power and re-trims to a lower angle of attack, the aircraft will accelerate so long as the thrust is greater than the drag, but the Square Law applies (Figure 138).

As the velocity increases, the drag force rises in proportion to the square of the speed. If the speed is doubled, the drag increases by four times. (As the velocity approaches the speed of sound in air, this is no longer true. The drag increases even more rapidly, as explained in a later chapter.) Whatever the power of the motor, the drag rises to equal the thrust and then the forces balance again; lift equals weight (together with any tail load), thrust equals drag. Equilibrium is restored, but at a higher speed. The aeroplane will reach its maximum speed, in level flight, when the engine is giving all the power it can.

In a dive, gravity will increase the airspeed. If an aeroplane is first climbed to a great height and then dived vertically, it will accelerate until the drag equals the total weight plus the thrust. When the forces are balanced in this way, the aircraft is in equilibrium again even though diving at a very great velocity. The speed will be constant. This is called a *terminal velocity* dive because the aircraft cannot be made to go any faster (Figure 139). Not many aircraft are

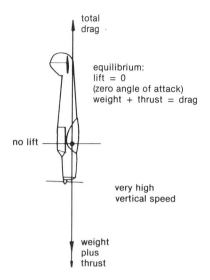

139. A terminal velocity dive.

strong enough to withstand the strains created by such a dive. There is, for each aircraft type, a speed known to pilots as the *red line* or *VNE* (velocity never to be exceeded). Often there is an actual red line marked on the airspeed indicator, and if the pilot flies any faster than this, the aircraft will possibly be damaged and may even break up. Of course a terminal velocity dive involves a very rapid loss of altitude, and unless started very high, the aircraft will hit the ground before reaching its maximum possible speed.

The development of the modern aeroplane

In the earlier aeroplanes, which had engines of low power, it was necessary to construct the whole aircraft very lightly because the motors could only drive the wing forward slowly and not much lift could be generated. Since the speeds were low, drag did not seem very important. The easiest way to make a very light, yet very strong, wing, is to copy the Hargrave box kite. *Biplanes* have a very large wing area and can give plenty of lift at low speeds. Between the planes, struts and bracing wires may be used to make the structure rigid. *Triplanes* were built. They were successful as fighters when they first appeared because they were very light and strong and so could climb rapidly and turn or loop sharply. These were advantages in combat, but because of the extra drag they were

slower than the biplane fighters. In the end speed proved more important. It was often vital to have a small speed advantage over the enemy to get into an attacking position or to escape when being pursued. Some designers even tried four and five wings, one above the other, to get the largest wing area for the least weight possible. Such aircraft flew quite well but very slowly, and proved to be of little use. As engines improved, higher speeds became possible and it became important to get rid of the drag of the struts and wires, and other things like undercarriages, open cockpits and square, boxy fuselages. Because of the greater speed, wings of smaller area could generate enough lift to carry the same or even greater loads. Both drag and lift obeyed the Square Law relative to airspeed.

New materials also became available (Figure 140). The earlier aeroplanes had light, wooden frameworks covered with fine quality light linen or cotton fabric. The fabric

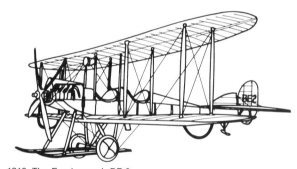

1913: The Farnborough BE 2.
Built from wood, covered with light fabric, braced with struts and wires.

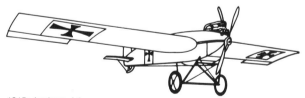

1915: Junkers J-1.
The first all-metal aeroplane, a monoplane with few external struts.

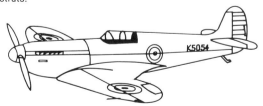

1936: The Supermarine Spitfire 1. All metal with a stressed skin, very carefully streamlined.

140. How aircraft changed from 1913 to 1936.

was 'doped' and painted or varnished to make it airtight. Later it was found better to build frameworks from aluminium alloys or thin-walled steel tubing. These were stronger than wood in relation to their weight, so a metal airframe could be both stronger and lighter than a wooden one. Wing and fuselage could be covered with thin alloy sheets, riveted on. The metal skin could be made to carry some of the bending and twisting stress, whereas fabric covering added no strength. Although wooden and fabric aeroplanes are still built, all-metal structures with stressed skins are by far the most usual now. Plastic materials are also becoming important, especially when reinforced with glass, carbon or other man-made types of fibre.

Except for special purposes where the abilities to fly slowly and carry heavy loads are required, modern aeroplanes are monoplanes and have no external struts or bracing wires. The fuselages are made smooth and carefully streamlined. Undercarriages retract, cockpits are enclosed and the whole structure is made as smooth as possible. All this is to reduce the drag to enable the aircraft to fly fast without excessive power. The high speed enables the monoplane wing to carry plenty of load, so aeroplanes have become not only more streamlined but also heavier. They need larger aerodromes to work from and often long, smooth, runways are essential to enable them to get up to take-off speed and to roll to a stop after landing.

Propellers

Until just before World War II, except for a few rather dangerous experiments with rocket drive, all aeroplanes had propellers to convert the power of their engines into

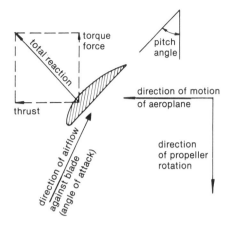

Each propeller blade behaves like a wing. Lift becomes thrust, drag becomes torque, if the total reaction is resolved relative to the direction of flight.

142. A propeller is like a rotating wing.

thrust. The propeller is sometimes called the airscrew, because it is rather like a woodscrew which moves forward as it turns.

An ordinary fan, such as those used for ventilation, is a kind of propeller. The fan is intended to remain in one place and propels the air to create a draught. If such a fan is free to move as it spins, it will drive itself along. This can be demonstrated by clamping an electric fan, with a long power lead, to a skateboard or any other free-wheeling trolley (Figure 141). Boats and hovercraft are frequently driven in this way, and it is possible to make a propeller-driven land vehicle.

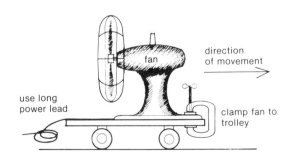

An electric fan may be used to drive a wheeled trolley. Aircraft propellers work in a similar way.

141. A fan used as a propeller.

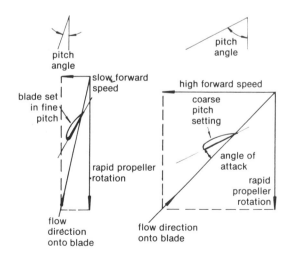

For take-off the propeller should be set in fine pitch. At high flying speeds a coarse pitch is required.

143. Adjusting the pitch of a propeller.

It is best to think of a propeller or fan blade as a rotating wing (Figure 142). Most domestic fans have blades of very low aspect ratio. Aeroplane propellers have much higher aspect ratios. Each blade is set at an angle to the hub. This is called the *pitch* of the propeller. The blades are shaped in section like a wing. As the propellor turns, each blade generates a force like the lift of a wing, but directed forwards. Like a windmill, the propeller blade has to be twisted to keep the angle of attack to the airflow nearly constant all the way along the blade. On early aeroplanes the propeller was often carved from laminated wood. Several thin planks of very good quality timber were glued together and afterwards carved to shape, varnished and polished.

When metal propellers became more common, they were usually mounted on special gears so that the pitch could be changed according to the pilot's needs. At take-off, the engine is giving maximum power (Figure 143). The propeller is turning very fast but the aeroplane moves forward slowly at first. This requires a fine *pitch* setting for the propeller. Once flying at high speed the propeller should be set to coarse pitch. This is because the direction of the flow across each blade changes as the forward speed of the whole propeller increases. On many aeroplanes a constant speed propeller is used. The blade pitch is adjusted automatically to give the most efficient angle of attack whatever the speed of flight. If for any reason the engine stops in flight, a variable pitch propeller can be feathered, with its blades set in line with the airflow. In this position they give least drag. A multi-engined aircraft can then usually continue flying on its remaining engines. A single engined aeroplane with a feathered propeller will glide more efficiently than if the propeller is stopped with its blades still facing the flow at an angle.

Model aircraft with twisted rubber motors often have folding propellers which lie flat against the fuselage when the rubber has given all its power. They then become efficient gliders. Variable pitch propeller blades may also be turned to a negative pitch. They will then give reversed thrust, tending to push the aeroplane backwards. This is very useful when landing. The reversed thrust acts as a powerful brake to shorten the landing run after touchdown.

144   Model aeroplanes are often powered by rubber motors. They turn large propellers, which fold flat after the rubber has given all its power, and the model becomes a sailplane.

The slipstream

The addition of a whirling propeller in front of an aeroplane wing and fuselage makes the airflow much more complicated than it is on a sailplane. Some aeroplanes, like the Wrights' biplanes, have the propellers mounted behind the wing. There are also some aircraft with propellers at the rear end of the fuselage. These act in much the same way as a water screw on a ship, the thrust pushes the craft along and the propeller wake is left behind. The *pusher propeller* does allow the fuselage and wing to work in smooth airflow, which creates rather less drag (Figure 145). For this reason some modern aeroplanes are arranged in this way although there are difficulties. Placing the engine and propeller behind tends to make the aircraft 'tail heavy', the wing has to be moved well back and all other heavy items such as fuel tanks, pilot and passengers or cargo, have to be moved forward to achieve balance. It is also rather difficult to arrange for a good flow of air to cool the engine if it is of the simplest, air-cooled type.

With the front-mounted or *tractor propeller*, the aircraft is pulled along. Designers have nearly always used the tractor arrangement. The balance problem is much easier, and all the heavy items can be grouped closer together than with the pusher layout.

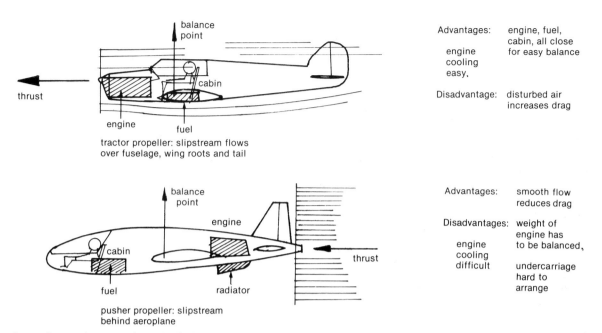

balance
point

cabin

thrust

engine   fuel

tractor propeller: slipstream flows
over fuselage, wing roots and tail

Advantages: engine, fuel,
                cabin, all close
engine   for easy balance
cooling
easy,

Disadvantage: disturbed air
                increases drag

balance
point

engine

cabin

thrust

fuel   radiator

pusher propeller: slipstream
behind aeroplane

Advantages: smooth flow
                 reduces drag

Disadvantages: weight of
                 engine has
engine   to be balanced,
cooling
difficult   undercarriage
                 hard to
                 arrange

A propeller may be arranged as a 'pusher' or a 'tractor'. Both types have advantages but most designers have used the 'tractor' type.

145. 'Pusher' and 'tractor' propellers.

The wake behind a rotating propeller tends to swirl round, creating a turbulent slipstream. The slipstream flows aft faster than the undisturbed air. In aeroplanes where there is an ordinary tail unit some distance behind the propeller, the slipstream gives the pilot more control because the faster flow over the rudder and elevator makes for a quicker response. At the same time, the slipstream tends to swing the tail (Figure 146). There is a sideways force on the fin and rudder because the slipstream strikes them at an angle. Many single-engined propeller-driven aeroplanes tend to swing quite sharply during take-off because of this, and pilots need to take care in keeping the aircraft running straight. This problem tends to be worse on small aeroplanes with very large, powerful engines, like the fighters used in World War II. The propellers had to be very large in diameter, which required the undercarriage to be long and stalky to keep the tips off the ground. Sometimes two propellers were used, mounted on the same axis, one behind the other, but rotating in opposite directions. This made control easier and allowed more powerful engines to be used without having to use even longer undercarriages. Where there are two or four engines, mounted on the wings in pairs, the

slipstream usually clears the tail. The swinging effect is less likely, but the tail may need to be larger to keep control in the slower airstream. Some propeller-driven aeroplanes have twin tails, to keep the fin and rudder in the slipstream for quicker control response.

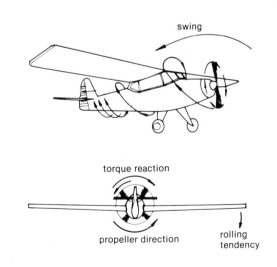

swing

torque reaction

propeller direction   rolling
                           tendency

The slipstream striking the fin may cause the aeroplane to swing to one side, and propeller torque tends to make it roll over.

146. Effects of torque and slipstream on an aircraft.

Another factor that causes aeroplanes to swing sometimes when the engine is at high power, is *torque* (Figure 146). The engine turns the propeller against the air resistance. There is a reaction from the air against the direction of the rotation, which tends to roll the aeroplane over. This is easily controlled by the ailerons and rudder, but it becomes very much more serious when propellers are very large, as in helicopters. This will be mentioned again in the next chapter.

Large propellers also have a gyroscopic effect. As the aeroplane changes its angle of attack during take-off, the gyroscopic force tends to swing the nose sideways. This is exactly the same effect as that which causes boomerangs to follow a circular flight path.

Trying to fly faster

By the time of World War II, propeller-driven aeroplanes were capable of flying faster than 600 km/h. More and more powerful engines were developed, but it become increasingly difficult to get extra speed. Because of the Square Law, to achieve even a small improvement in speed a very large increase in thrust was needed. Adding more engines did not prove to be the answer, because more engines added more weight and needed more fuel; the whole aeroplane then had to be bigger, with larger wings, tail and fuselage and so more drag. In the end the maximum speed reached was not greater than the single-engined aircraft. The best propeller-driven fighters reached speeds up to about 780 km/h. A very few special experimental types managed 800 km/h.

The main problem was not lack of engine power, but the propeller. When an aeroplane is flying at its maximum speed, the outer tips of the propeller blades are moving through the air faster than any other part of the aircraft (Figure 147). This is because they are moving along with the whole aeroplane but at the same time rotating very rapidly. The propeller tip follows a helical path and its speed is a combination of forward and rotational speeds. It was shown in the chapter on windmills that a large wind turbine turning at only a few revolutions per minute can exceed the speed of sound at the outer tips. Aeroplane propellers turn much faster than windmill sails, and on a fast-moving aircraft the tips soon approach sonic speed. The drag of the propeller increases greatly. Severe vibrations

The propeller tips move much faster through the air than any other part of the aeroplane. They may approach the speed of sound.

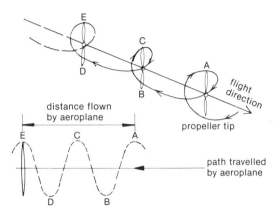

As the aeroplane moves from A to E, the propeller tips follow a much longer path from A through B, C, D to E in the same time.

147. Speed of the propeller tips.

begin if the blades are made to turn any faster. The strain on the engine and the whole airframe is enormous and the structure may begin to break up. Even some slow transport aircraft had propeller tips which operated quite near sonic speed, and created a great deal of very unpleasant noise. It was becoming impossible to get propeller-driven aeroplanes to fly any faster. In more recent times, propeller design has advanced to some extent. The cross sections of the blades have been improved and the outer parts may be swept back. It is still not possible to use a propeller for thrust in very high speed flight.

Things to do:

1   Try the experiment with electric fan and wheeled trolley that was mentioned in the text. With battery power, or a model aeroplane propeller driven by a small motor, a propeller-driven land vehicle or boat may be made.

2   Adapt a small model glider to take a rubber motor and propeller, along the lines of Penaud's model of 1871 (Figure 148). When trying to fly the model, be prepared for turning effects caused by the slipstream and torque, especially if the propeller is a tractor type. Arrange for a demonstration of a powered model aeroplane. A local model aircraft club will usually be glad to co-operate.

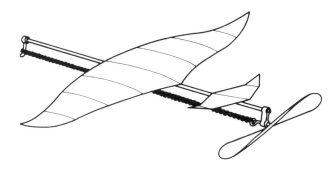

As early as 1871, a simple rubber-driven propeller was fitted to a model glider, which flew successfully. The designer was Alphonse Penaud. In this case the propeller was of the 'pusher' type.

148. A glider designed in 1871 by Alphonse Penaud.

Study the motor and the propeller used. Join a model aero club and learn how to build and fly powered models as well as gliders.

3   Visit an aerodrome and compare the different types of propeller-driven aircraft. Ask to be shown a variable-pitch airscrew.

4   Short flights in light aeroplanes are often available, for a fee, and with parental permission if you are a minor.

Things to find out:

1   Find out all you can about the early trials with powered flight before 1903. Some names to look up as well as the Wrights: Alphonse Penaud, Clement Ader, Hiram Maxim, Samuel Langley.

2   Read about early aviation in Australia, and try to decide who was truly the first to fly an aeroplane. Remember that flight under full control is what counts.

3   Study the early aviators who made record-breaking flights. Some to look for in addition to those mentioned in the text are Louis Bleriot, Claude Graham-White, Albert Read (US Navy), Richard Byrd, Alan Cobham, Charles Lindbergh, Jean Batten, Amelia Earhart, Wiley Post, Jim Mollison, Hubert Wilkins. There are many more.

4   The Schneider Trophy Races for seaplanes began before the First World War, and continued until 1931. Find pictures and drawings of the winning aircraft in each race and compare them. Try to explain how the speeds in the race were increased.

5   Read about the MacRobertson Air Race from Britain to Australia in 1934.

6   Collect pictures or drawings of world air speed record aircraft up to 1947.

7   Study the history of airlines in Australia from their beginnings. What types of aeroplane were used and how did they change as time went on?

chapter 11

helicopters

The idea of flying without wings by means of an airscrew is very old indeed. Long before anyone had built a successful glider it was discovered that a small set of blades from a toy windmill could be made to rise into the air by being rotated rapidly. Using feathers stuck into corks for the blades, and strips of springy wood or whalebone for power, little helicopters could be made to fly quite well (Figure 149). When the power from the spring was used up they would fall to the ground. In nature, the seeds of some trees like the sycamore showed that a turning blade could safely carry a load down. Some of the first attempts to fly were made with pedal driven helicopters, but they always failed and the success of gliders and aeroplanes caused the helicopter to be forgotten for some time.

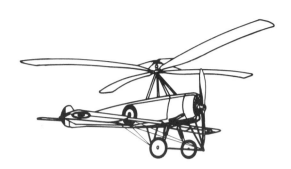

Jokingly called 'the flying windmill', the autogiro was pulled along by a normal motor with a tractor airscrew. The main lifting rotor span round like a windmill, without engine drive.

150. De la Cierva's autogiro of 1926.

Such models were known for at least 150 years before a man-carrying helicopter was flown successfully.

149. A toy helicopter powered by a strip of whale bone.

De la Cierva's autogiro

A few people did continue experiments. Juan De la Cierva invented a flying machine called the *autogiro* (Figure 150). This was not a true helicopter but it did have a rotating wing. The autogiro was jokingly called the flying windmill. There was a motor at the front with an ordinary propeller which pulled the aircraft through the air. The main rotor was set with its axle tilted slightly backwards. The forward movement caused the rotor to turn in the same way as a simple fan will turn if it is in a moving airstream. The autogiro rotor was held at a fine angle to the flow, rather than facing it squarely like a windmill, but the cause of the rotation was the same. Each

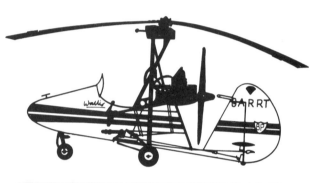

The modern gyrocopter uses the autogiro principle. The airscrew is arranged as a pusher.

151. The gyrocopter.

part of the rotor was shaped like a narrow wing and the lift from the blades enabled the autogiro to fly. To take off, De la Cierva could taxi out like an ordinary aeroplane, and accelerate rapidly forwards. The rotor would begin to blow round and soon would lift the aircraft off the ground. To get the rotor spinning fast enough to take off required a long run across the ground. To make the autogiro more useful, De la Cierva arranged a system of gears and shafts so that he could drive the main rotor round rapidly while standing still. When he was ready to take off he would disconnect the drive to the rotor and transfer all the power to the tractor propeller. The autogiro could then take off after a very short run. Once in the air the rotor kept on turning because the front propeller kept the autogiro moving forwards. To land, it was possible to settle down almost vertically with the rotor 'windmilling' or 'auto-rotating'. The autogiro needed very little space to land. If the engine failed it could glide down into almost any small area without damage.

Today the autogiro principle is still used for small *gyrocopters* (Figure 150 and Photo 151). It is also possible to make a kite with an auto-rotating wing. Man-carrying kites of this kind were used during World War II for aerial spotting from submarines. They may also be used for power generation (see also Figure 184).

The first helicopters

It was natural for people to want to improve on the autogiro by driving the rotor from the engine all the time. This would enable vertical take-off and landing, and hovering flight, as well as forward motion. The autogiro was always slow, because the rotor caused a lot of drag. With a power drive, the rotor itself could be used to lift and at the same time pull the helicopter forward. This would require the axis to be tilted forwards instead of back. The first problem was torque. To turn a large lifting rotor round at sufficient speed to create lift sets up a strong air resistance. The reaction on the body of the aircraft is to turn it round in the opposite direction to the rotor. Some of the early attempts to make a helicopter fly found the engine and fuselage spinning round just as fast, or even faster, than the rotor.

The first successful helicopter was the Focke-Achgelis flown by Hanna Reitsch in Germany in 1936 (Figure 152). This solved the torque difficulty by having two rotors going in opposite directions. Each rotor was mounted on a long outrigger at the side, to prevent them striking one another as they

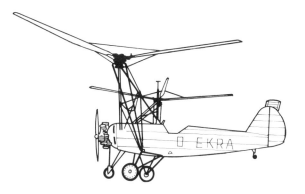

The two rotors were driven around by the main engine. Vertical take-off and hovering flight were possible.

152. The first successful helicopter, flown by Hanna Reitsch in 1936.

One of Igor Sikorsky's early helicopters with a tail rotor to counteract torque and cyclic pitch change of the main lifting rotor blades.

153. A Sikorsky helicopter.

spun round. With this aircraft Hanna was able to take off and fly round inside a large indoor sports hall, and land again safely in front of a huge crowd of spectators. Helicopters with two rotors are still used, especially to lift heavy loads.

Igor Sikorsky, a Russian who later settled in America, solved the torque problem by using a small second rotor, at the tail, to keep the fuselage from turning (Figure 153). Most modern helicopters use this system now. The idea was rather like the fantail rotor of a windmill. The small rotor's job is to keep the body of the mill, or helicopter, pointing in the desired direction.

A further great difficulty was that when a helicopter is moving forwards the blades on one side are moving at a different speed from those on the other. On one side, the rotor travels through the air at the speed of rotation plus the speed of the helicopter's flight. On the other side the blades move at the rotation speed minus the helicopter's speed. The

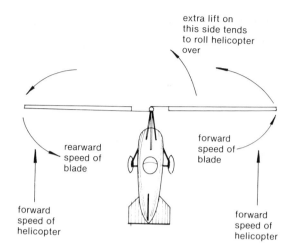

The extra lift caused by the forward speed of flight tended to turn the whole aircraft over or force it into a boomerang flight path.

154. Why early helicopters failed.

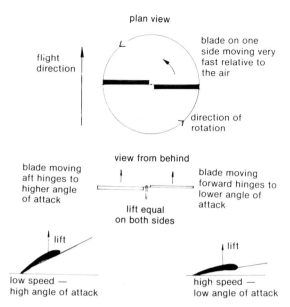

The blades of a helicopter rotor are free to hinge and flap to a certain extent. The angle of attack changes automatically as each blade sweeps round, thus equalising the lift, even when the helicopter is moving forward through the air. In addition, the pilot's control column is connected, through a system of rods and levers, to the rotor in such a way that the angle of each blade can be changed to vary the lift as required to tilt the rotor.

155. Cyclic pitch control.

lift from any wing-like blade depends on the speed at which it moves through the air, and the angle of attack. (The Square Law operates.) The difference in the lifting force on the right and left side of a single rotor, caused by the differences in speed, was enough to turn some early experimental helicopters completely upside down as soon as they began to fly forwards (Figure 154). This is a similar effect to that which tends to turn a boomerang upside down in flight.

The solution was to change the angle of attack of each blade as it swept round (Figure 155). This required each blade to change its pitch at the hub, at each part of its rotation. The mechanism, known as *cyclic pitch control*, is what makes the modern single-rotor helicopter possible. The blades are either hinged so that they can change pitch as they go round, or the inner part of the blade is made flexible without any actual hinge, so that it can twist and bend to the required angles. Either way, the lift on the two sides is made equal automatically. The hingeing, or flexibility, of the rotor blades explains why they droop downwards when the helicopter is standing on the ground. In flight they ride upwards.

To steer the helicopter it is necessary to tilt the whole rotor in the desired direction (Figure 156). This can be done without changing the direction of the fuselage, so helicopters can move sideways or backwards. If

the rotor axis is upright a helicopter will hover.

If the motor fails, the helicopter can descend very much like an autogiro, with its rotor 'windmilling' or auto-rotating. There is an unpleasant fall for some distance before the blades can take up their new position, so if the failure is near the ground an accident is likely, but if there is enough height the pilot can usually glide down to the nearest open space and touch down safely.

Several factors prevent helicopters from flying as fast as aeroplanes. On one side, as the blades rotate, their speed through the air is greater than the speed of the whole helicopter. As mentioned before, this increases the lift on this side unless the blade can change its angle of attack. On the other side the rotor blades move backwards and their speed through the air is slower. The angle of attack on that side has to be increased to maintain equal lift on the two sides. Unfortunately, if any wing-like surface is at too high an angle of attack, it will stall. The faster the helicopter flies forward, the more the rearward-turning blades have to increase

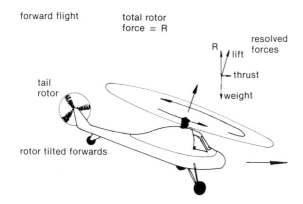

forward flight

total rotor force = R

resolved forces

R — lift
— thrust
weight

tail rotor

rotor tilted forwards

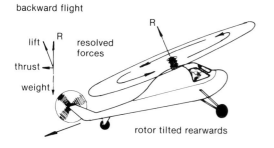

backward flight

lift — R — resolved forces

thrust —

weight

R

rotor tilted rearwards

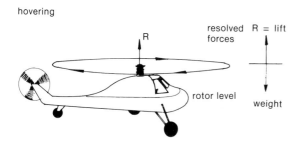

hovering

R

resolved forces   R = lift

rotor level

weight

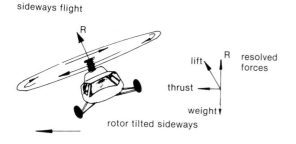

sideways flight

R

lift — R — resolved forces

thrust —

weight

rotor tilted sideways

By varying the angle of attack of each blade of the rotor, to make the lift on one side or the other more, the pilot can make the entire rotor, with the helicopter below it, tilt slightly. This allows the aircraft to move in any direction or, by bringing the rotor to the horizontal position, to hover.

156. Manoeuvring a helicopter.

157   The helicopter rotor is driven by the main engine. As this photograph shows, the hub of the rotor is quite complicated, and the blades are hinged to allow them to change angles as they rotate. Without this 'cyclic pitch control' the helicopter would not fly safely. (Adelaide *Advertiser*)

their lift, but eventually they reach the stalling angle. The helicopter then will be unable to fly properly. This is the speed limit for this type of aircraft.

Another limit is set by the speed of sound. Like a windmill, the tips of a helicopter rotor move more rapidly than the inner parts of the blades. The blades moving through the forward side of the rotation travel through the air very fast indeed. Their speed is the speed of the whole aircraft plus the speed due to the rotation. When flying at maximum speed the tips on modern helicopters are already close to sonic speed. If they were driven any faster a helicopter would produce a rapid series of sonic bangs as each blade swept round. Apart from the very unpleasant noise, like gunfire, the shock waves would cause damage to the aircraft and possibly to things on the ground beneath as well. The steady beating noise made by helicopters is an indication that the blade tips are working at very high speeds.

Hovercraft, like helicopters, have a rotor or fan, but the purpose is not to lift the craft directly. The fan acts as a blower to create a cushion of air underneath the hull, lifting it just clear of the ground or water surface. Flexible curtains are usually fixed all round to prevent the air flowing out too quickly at the sides of the vehicle. Propulsion is usually provided by large airscrews. The advantage of such vehicles is that they can move easily over water, swamp or land without special roads or tracks.

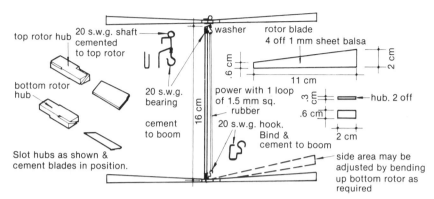

Note that lower rotor has opposite pitch to upper rotor.
Pitch adjustment obtained by carefully warping blades.
Increase in pitch gives increased rate of climb.

158. A simple rubber-driven twin-rotor helicopter model.

Things to do:

1   Make a small two-rotor helicopter, using a rubber motor, as suggested in Figure 158. It should be possible to make it climb straight up for some distance but it will fall when the motor stops. Remove the lower rotor and try to fly it with only one. What happens, and why?

2   Study a model radio-controlled helicopter and learn how it is made to fly.

3   Arrange to visit a local helicopter base and find out as much as possible about the aircraft. Study the rotor and controls with special attention. Flights in helicopters are sometimes available.

Things to find out:

1   What are helicopters used for? What advantages do they have for these tasks over ordinary aeroplanes? How much do they cost to operate, and how does this compare with aeroplanes?

2   What are the speed and height records for helicopters?

3   Collect pictures of some early experiments with helicopters and explain why they did not fly very well.

4   Read about the careers of Igor Sikorsky and Hanna Reitsch.

chapter 12

rocket and jet propulsion

The idea of propelling an aircraft by rocket or some kind of jet is very old, but no practical way of making engines of either kind was discovered until propeller-driven aeroplanes were already flying successfully.

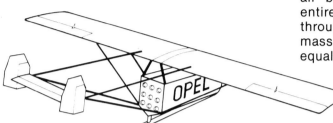

Nine powder-filled rockets were used. Once ignited there was no means of shutting off the power.

159. Fritz von Opel's rocket-powered glider which flew in 1929.

Fritz von Opel tried a rocket-propelled glider in 1929 (Figure 159). He reached a good speed of about 160 km/h, but the rockets were of the powder-fuelled type and were almost impossible to control. There was a great deal of heat, smoke and flame which scorched the glider. Once fired, there was no means of turning off the power and once burned out, no means of re-lighting.

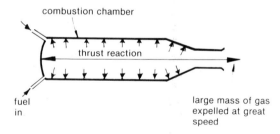

In a modern liquid-fuelled rocket motor the thrust can be controlled by varying the amount of fuel injected into the combustion chamber.

160. Reaction thrust.

A rocket is a *reaction thrust* engine. The fuel, which may be in solid, powder or liquid form, is burned inside a container which has a nozzle. The burning creates a very large amount of hot gas which expands. The pressure inside the chamber becomes very high, the gas thrusting out in all directions (Figure 160). If the combustion chamber is not very strong it will burst. Since the rocket motor has an escape nozzle, a large mass of

gas is pushed out at very high speed. There is an equally strong reaction which thrusts the combustion chamber, and anything attached to it, in the other direction. This has nothing to do with the exhaust pushing against the air behind the rocket, the thrust comes entirely from the rapid ejection of gas through the tail nozzle. To push any large mass away in one direction produces an equal and opposite thrust.

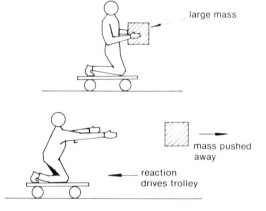

Reaction thrust may be demonstrated by pushing a large mass away while standing or kneeling on a wheeled trolley or skateboard.

161. Reaction thrust.

It is easy to understand reaction thrust if a few simple experiments are done on a skateboard, roller, or ice skates. If someone stands on a skateboard holding a heavy bag or some other large mass, and then throws the bag away, there is a reaction which causes the skater to roll away in the opposite direction (Figure 161). The harder and faster the mass is pushed away, the more the thrust reaction. The rocket motor works in the same general way. A rocket will thus provide thrust in a vacuum or near-vacuum, which is why such motors are needed for space vehicles.

A jet engine of the kind used on many modern aeroplanes also produces its thrust by reaction. A large mass of gas is heated to make it expand and rush out of the rear nozzle. In this case the gas is air, which has to be drawn in at the front of the motor. A jet engine will not work in a vacuum, but for flight within the atmosphere it provides very powerful reactive thrust.

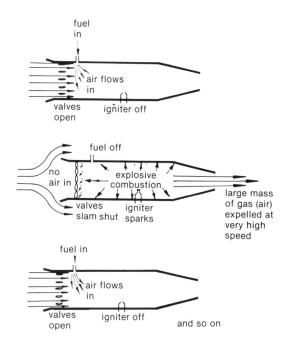

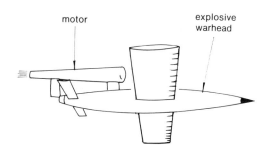

163. The pulse-jet powered flying bombs launched against London during World War II.

162. The pulse-jet engine.

The turbojet engine

The modern *turbojet engine* is more elaborate but capable of very large thrust (Figure 164). It is both quieter than the pulse jet and more economical. At the front of the engine is an air intake, which has to be carefully shaped to make a smooth channel into the engine. A bad intake form would slow the air down too much. Inside the engine the air is drawn into a *compressor*. The most usual type of compressor is like a series of fans with many small blades, one behind the other, which takes the air from the intake and forces it into a much smaller volume before passing it into the combustion chamber. In the combustion chamber the liquid fuel is forced in through nozzles, and burns with very great heat. Unlike the pulse jet, the flame is continuous. The compressed air expands enormously due to the heat, and streams out through the tail nozzle at very great speed. On the way, it passes through the blades of the turbine, which is another fan-like arrangement of blades, connected to the compressor by a shaft. A turbine is really a small windmill in a tunnel, which is blown

The pulse jet engine

The *pulse jet engine*, which was used to power the V1 flying bombs in World War II, relied on air entering the combustion chamber through a series of flap valves at the front of the motor (Figure 162).

Fuel was squirted into the chamber and ignited by a spark plug. The flash of flame heated the air which expanded almost explosively. The valves at the front were automatically slammed shut by the sudden expansion, so the only direction for the hot air to move was backwards out through the tail nozzle. The reaction pushed the aircraft forward. As soon as one lot of fuel was burned, the valves would spring open again, more air entered, and another injection of fuel gave another expansion and so on. These motors were cheap to make and produced good thrust, but were very noisy and used a great deal of fuel. In wartime that did not matter much (Figure 163). These pilotless aircraft flew faster than all but the very best of the propeller-driven fighters sent to shoot them down.

Some model aeroplanes have flown, on control lines, with miniature pulse jet motors. They are very fast but almost unbearably noisy.

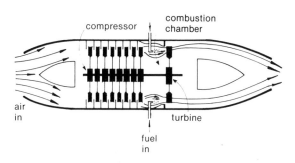

164. The turbojet engine.

round at very great speed by the fast airstream flowing through. (Water and steam turbines work in the same fashion.) It is because the jet of hot air spins the turbine to drive the compressor that these engines are called turbojet engines.

In designing a turbojet engine, the engineer has to consider the way in which air flows all the way through the motor. As it passes through the compressor stage, the air is not only compressed but also swirled round in a vortex. This continues inside the combustion chamber and affects the way the fuel burns. The very high temperature of the air passing through the turbine at great velocity requires special material to be used for the blades, which also must be shaped in such a way that they will extract enough power to turn the compressor without slowing the air jet down too much. As the air leaves the tail nozzle, it is still very hot and must not be allowed to flow over any part of the aircraft's structure.

In some turbojet engines, some of the intake air is allowed to bypass the combustion chamber. This cooler air is then mixed with the hot jet, giving a larger mass of air moving at slower speed. This is quieter and, for commercial airliners, provides good thrust with less use of fuel. Many jet motors are also fitted with afterburners, which allow some extra fuel to be burned in the tail pipe. This heats the air even more and gives the jet extra volume and speed. The afterburner is used only when a large surge of extra power is needed.

The first successful turbojet motor was designed by Frank Whittle, a British Royal Air Force engineer officer. It first operated in 1937, but it was four years before Whittle was able to have such an engine tested in a real aeroplane, a special aircraft built by the Gloster Aircraft Company. By that time, in Germany Hans von Ohain had also produced a turbojet, and his engine was actually flying successfully a few days before World War II broke out. His test aircraft, the He 178, built by Heinkel, took off on August 27th 1939 (Figure 165). The German Luftwaffe was able to get two different jet aircraft types into action just before the end of the war with a very fast rocket-powered fighter as well. The RAF, at almost the same time, introduced the Gloster Meteor but by the end of the war still had only this one type of jet fighter in service. It was not long before nearly all military aircraft were jet-powered.

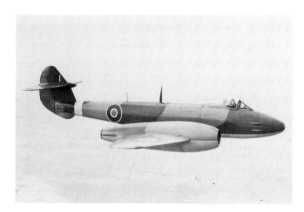

166   One of the first successful jet aircraft, the Gloster Meteor, which broke speed records in 1946. (Associated Press)

The gas turbine motor

The turbojet works best at high velocities. At moderate speeds and heights, propellers are more efficient. It took some years for commercial airliners to be developed to take advantage of the new motors. A first stage was to use a turbojet motor to drive a propeller. This required a larger turbine which could take nearly all the power from the jet and use it to turn not only the compressor but the propeller shaft as well. Some reaction thrust was produced, too. Such *turboprop engines* are still used on medium-sized airliners such as the Fokker Friendship, and on some smaller aircraft. Gas turbines have also been used to power cars, railway trains and ships and in some circumstances may be useful to drive dynamos for electric power generation.

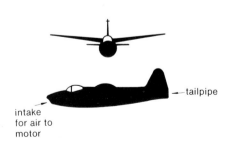

intake
for air to
motor

tailpipe

The Heinkel 178 was the first turbojet-powered aeroplane to fly. It took off in 1939.

165. Heinkel 178.

167   The Boeing 747, a large jet-powered aeroplane, showing the swept-back wings and tail unit. (Cathay Pacific)

The jet airliner

The first turbojet-powered airliner was the De Havilland Comet, which flew in 1949 and entered passenger service in 1952. Within a few years, all major international airliners were jet-powered, flying much higher and faster than the propeller-driven types. It has now become quite unusual to travel in any other way over long distances.

Most airliners allow the jet thrust to be reversed, just as some propeller-driven aeroplanes could reverse the pitch of the blades to slow down the landing run. The tailpipe contains a system of vanes and scoops which turn the bulk of the jet round and force it to blow forwards. The reaction slows the aircraft down rapidly. In some aircraft it is also possible to turn the thrust downwards to enable an aircraft to take off vertically, like a helicopter. The aeroplane may be fitted with additional engines mounted upright so that the thrust from these motors is always straight down. These 'lift' engines are shut off when in level flight under the thrust of a normal motor, and are then just so much extra load for the aircraft to carry, which is rather wasteful. A more economical system is for the tail pipes of the ordinary thrust engines to be made to swivel, turning the jet downwards. The upward reaction supports the weight. Small jets are directed to the sides to rotate the aeroplane, or to correct any tilting caused by gusts of wind. Such a jet aircraft can rise from a small launching pad or from the deck of a ship, ascend vertically to a suitable height, and then, by turning some of the thrust backwards again, start moving forward. As the forward speed increases, the wings begin to produce lift in the usual way, and more of the jet thrust can be directed aft to increase the speed until the wings do all the lifting and the jet motor provides only horizontal thrust. To land, the procedure is the other way round and the 'jump-jet' can settle down vertically into a small space. The Hawker Siddeley Harrier military aircraft operates in this way.

Things to do:

1   It is dangerous to experiment with rockets and jet motors without qualified assistance and supervision. There are model rocket kits available and in some areas there are model rocket clubs. It is strongly recommended that anyone wishing to experiment should join such a club.

2   Arrange, if possible, to visit an aircraft maintenance workshop to see a turbojet engine at close quarters. Alternatively, such

motors are often displayed in transport or science and technological museums.

Things to find out:

1   Find drawings and photographs of the earliest jet aircraft built in Germany and Britain.

2   Find out as much as possible about the Messerschmitt 163, a small rocket-driven fighter aircraft used in World War II.

3   Read about the development of rockets from the earliest times to the present day.

4   Read the story of Frank Whittle, inventor of the turbojet.

chapter 13

supersonic
flights

In 1946 the Gloster Meteor set new speed records, reaching 991 km/h (Photo 166). Soon afterwards 1000 km/h was exceeded by newer jet-powered aircraft. More powerful turbojet motors were built and pilots looked ahead to flying faster than sound.

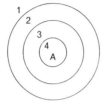

a. Sound from any source not moving, travels out in waves in all directions. The waves move at about 340m/sec at sea level.

b. If the source of the sound is moving, the waves crowd closer on one side and spread out on the other.

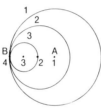

c. At the speed of sound the moving object keeps pace with its own sound waves, so the waves are unable to spread out ahead of it. A shock wave forms.

168. How a shock wave forms.

Sound travels through the air as waves. The speed of sound is the speed at which the waves travel (Figure 168). As each wave passes, the air particles move closer together and then further apart (Figure 169). These small variations of density and pressure cause the ear drums of a person to vibrate and the brain interprets this as a noise.

The movement of sound waves from the source of the noise is somewhat like the movement of ripples across a calm pond after a stone has been dropped into the water, but the water ripples are up-and-down movements at the surface. In air there is no such surface. Since the atmosphere varies in temperature and density, especially at different heights, the speed of sound is not the same everywhere. At sea level it is normally about 341 metres per second (1228 km/h). In cold weather sound travels more slowly and on hot days, faster. At an altitude of 3000 metres in the International Standard Atmosphere (see Chapter 1) it is about 328 m/sec

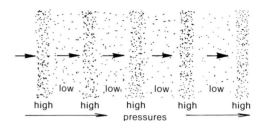

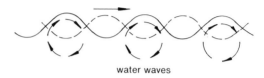

Sound waves are waves of pressure change, rather than up-and-down movements like waves on water.

169. Sound waves and water waves.

and at an altitude of 10 000 m, the height at which modern airliners often fly, sound travels about 300 m/sec (1080 km/h).

The Mach number

It is often much more important to know how close to the speed of sound the flight is, than to know the true airspeed. A convenient way of measurement is to use the *Mach number* (named after Ernst Mach, who invented it). To work out the Mach number, the actual airspeed is divided by the speed of sound at the height and temperature concerned. So if an aeroplane is flying at 1000 km/h at sea level, it will have a Mach number of about 1000/1228 = 0.81. Another way of putting this is to say the speed is 81 per cent of the speed of sound at sea level. At an altitude of 10 000 m, the flight speed of 1000 km/h represents a Mach number of 1000 ÷ 1080, which comes to about 0.93, or 93 per cent of the speed of sound. Jet airliners cruising at fairly normal airspeeds at this altitude are at Mach numbers between 0.75 and 0.85. A Mach number of 1.0 describes flight at the speed of sound and of course, M = 2.0 or 3.0 indicates speeds twice and three times faster than sound. The Concorde supersonic airliner flies at about Mach 2.0.

Even with propeller-driven aircraft, pilots sometimes ran into serious trouble at high speeds. It often happened that a fast and heavy fighter aeroplane, in a steep dive, would begin to shake violently, approaching Mach 0.6 or 0.7. Some broke up. When the turbojet motor allowed more thrust to be obtained in level flight, it was not long before these problems became much more severe. Several pilots were killed when their aircraft went out of control or disintegrated. It seemed as if there was a real bar to further increases in speed and people began to talk of 'the sound barrier'. Some thought supersonic flight for piloted aircraft would prove impossible.

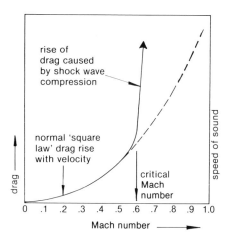

The drag of an aeroplane wing increases very rapidly once the critical Mach number for its shape is reached.

171. How the critical Mach number affects drag.

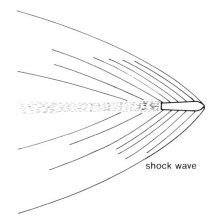

A bullet travelling at Mach 10 (ten times the speed of sound) creates shock waves which make a loud cracking sound as the projectile goes by.

170. Projectile shock waves.

Shock waves

Yet some things were already known to travel faster than sound. Bullets and projectiles from large guns do so (Figure 170). Ernst Mach himself, in 1873, had already described shock waves caused by projectiles, and quite a lot was known about the ways in which air behaved when things moved through it at such velocities.

During World War II, the first ballistic missiles, big rockets used to bombard London, travelled at supersonic speed. Those nearby who were lucky enough to survive the explosion, heard a long rumbling sound, like a peal of thunder, immediately after the arrival of the rocket. This was the sound of the missile, which continued to arrive for some seconds after the rocket itself had done the damage. At night it was also noticed that the missiles glowed red-hot during the last phases of their fall. They could be seen, but not heard, before they

arrived. The speed was great enough to cause heating of the rocket skin during flight.

All the studies of airflow which had enabled windmills, kites, gliders and aeroplanes to be designed, were based on the assumption that air was incompressible. It was always understood that this was not strictly correct, but at low Mach numbers, less than 0.5, it made very little difference and could be ignored for all practical purposes. At the higher Mach numbers reached by jet aircraft, the working theories have to be altered (Figure 171). The Square Law of drag and lift no longer applies. The drag at high Mach numbers increases very much more rapidly than the Square Law suggests, and lift tends to decrease.

At low speeds, air begins to feel the influence of anything moving through it, before the object arrives. The flow ahead of a lifting wing begins to divide in advance and passes over and under the wing without any shock. Near the speed of sound, the air is actually compressed by the very rapid approach of a wing, and a wave of denser, compressed air races forward just in front. It is the energy used to compress the air that causes the great rise in drag at Mach numbers above 0.6. As Mach 1 approaches, the compression wave becomes even sharper. Instead of having a warning the air is suddenly and sharply squeezed. The wave of compression cannot move ahead faster than the speed of sound.

When something travels through air faster than sound, the sharp compression wave becomes very intense indeed and is called a *shock wave.* To the ear, the passage of such a wave sounds like a sharp crack or bang. How loud the bang is depends on the speed and size of the object causing it. Soldiers who have been narrowly missed by rifle bullets often hear two apparent explosions: as the bullet goes by there is a crack caused by the shock wave, then the sound of the gun firing arrives. (By that time the soldier is safe from that shot, at least!) Small shock waves are common in everyday experience. Anything that forces air to move faster than sound creates a shock wave which people hear as a pop or bang. An explosion, whatever causes it in the first place, pushes the air out very sharply all round and sends a shock wave in all directions. When a door slams, the bang is actually a shock wave set off by the very sudden compression of the air from between the door and the frame just before the two meet.

On an aeroplane wing, the speed of the airflow, especially over the upper surface, is faster than the speed of flight. It is this increase of speed that creates the lift. When the whole aircraft is moving at a high Mach number, the air over the wings may reach Mach 1 even when the aeroplane itself is travelling only at Mach 0.7 or 0.8 (Figure 172). A small shock wave will then form above the wing. When this happens, the pressures over the wing change and the controls may no longer work correctly. The aeroplane may be thrown out of its normal trim. Behind the shock wave, the air tends to separate from the wing, causing great increase in drag. If this turbulent air strikes the tail, it may cause severe fluttering vibrations, all adding to the pilot's difficulties. It was for these reasons that many of the first very high-speed aircraft become uncontrollable as they approached the speed of sound.

New types of wing

The rather thick wings which proved very good on slower aircraft developed incipient shock waves at Mach numbers about 0.6. This was a critical figure for them. By making the wings much thinner, the critical Mach number could be raised. It was computed that wings which had their thickest point further back, with very carefully graded and smooth curves in cross section, would have even higher critical Mach numbers. New wings were developed, much thinner, with sharper leading edges and gently curved sections instead of the rather thick, bluntly rounded forms of the slower aircraft (Figure 173). The metal skins were made as smooth as possible, because any small bump can set up a local shock wave.

A most important discovery was that sweeping the wings back or forward increased the critical Mach number even more (Figure 174). All modern jet airliners have wings of the swept-back type. They cruise safely at Mach numbers above 0.7. Incipient shock waves do form on the wings. It is possible sometimes to see signs of these from the passenger cabin. If the aircraft is flying through very thin, high haze or cloud, with the sun in the right place, a faint, wavering line may sometimes be seen running along the wing, about one third of the way back from the leading edge. The compression of the air, which is very close to Mach 1, bends the light passing through and leaves this shadow. This is known as a schlieren effect and may be used in a wind tunnel to make shock waves visible. Special

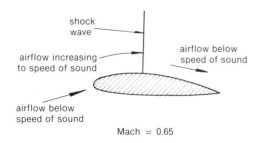

At the critical Mach number for a particular wing, a shock wave forms on the upper side, where the airflow reaches the speed of sound before the aircraft itself is at such a velocity.

172. Wing shock waves at sub-sonic aircraft speeds.

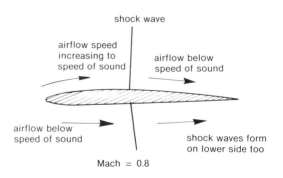

173. For speeds of flight above Mach 0.6, thinner wings with carefully designed shapes were needed. Even with these, shock waves form when the flow reaches the speed of sound above and below the wing.

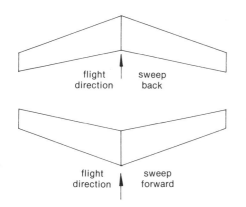

A wing which is swept back, or forward, has a higher critical Mach number than a straight wing. Most jet aircraft now have sweptback wings. To the air flowing over it, a swept wing appears thinner than a straight one.

174. Achieving a higher critical Mach number.

apparatus is used to increase the effect but it does occasionally occur in natural lighting.

At supersonic speeds, conditions are different again (Figure 175). The small shock wave on the wings moves further aft as the speed rises towards Mach 1, and in front of the aircraft there forms a bow shock wave. The faster the flight, the sharper the angle of these shock waves. The aircraft is constantly moving forward faster than the shock compression can travel.

People on the ground may see the supersonic aircraft passing over, but the first shock wave does not reach them until it is some distance beyond. When it does arrive they hear a sharp bang, followed, usually, by

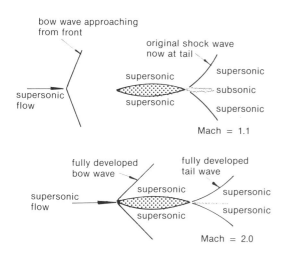

175. Shock waves at supersonic speeds form both in front of and behind a wing.

a second report as the other shockwave goes by. Then they hear the rumble which is the sound of the aeroplane. The loudness and sharpness of the *sonic bang* varies with the size and speed of the aircraft causing it, and the altitude. In a bad case, the shock wave can cause damage on the ground. For these reasons supersonic flight is often forbidden over populated regions.

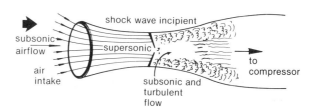

176. Shock waves may choke the air intake to a turbojet engine even at subsonic speeds.

Apart from the problems of wings and other external parts of the aeroplane, high speed flight causes difficulties for the air intake of a turbojet engine. Inside, shock waves form (Figure 176). These can choke the intake and starve the engine of air. After passing through the combustion chamber, the air is moving even faster and shock waves again may rob the jet of much of its power. The design of intakes and tail pipes for jet engines is thus a highly complicated matter. Since the shock is caused by compression of the air, and the compressor of a turbojet has to do exactly the same, it is possible to use the shock wave at the mouth of the intake to assist the compressor. After passing through the engine, shock waves tend to choke the exit. The nozzle may be flared out into a bell-like form, allowing the jet to expand gradually before escaping.

The ramjet engine

In a *ramjet engine*, there is no compressor and hence no need of a turbine (Figure 177). The motor consists of a very carefully shaped tube into which fuel is injected and burned. The forward movement itself compresses the air as it rushes into the pipe, it is then heated by the combustion of the fuel and rushes out of the tail, producing the high speed jet and forward reaction. There are no moving parts in the engine itself.

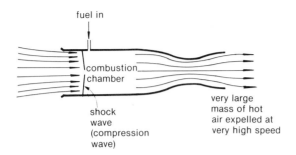

The ramjet engine relies on compression of the air in the intake, and requires no turbine. It must, however, be moving very fast before it can provide thrust.

177. Shock wave in a ramjet engine.

The great difficulty with such motors is that they obviously cannot work until they are already travelling very fast. To burn fuel inside a simple pipe standing still or moving slowly simply causes fire to pour out at both ends with no thrust at all. Some guided missiles have used ramjet motors. They are first launched and accelerated to great speeds by rockets. When the rockets have expired, the ramjet is moving fast enough for it to take over. Another application that has been tried is to drive a helicopter rotor. The ramjet motors are mounted at the outer ends of the blades and fuel is carried to them through tubes inside the blades. The rotor is first spun to a speed which allows the ramjets to operate, after which they quickly reach an efficient velocity while the helicopter itself may still be on the ground.

Problems with swept wings

A swept-back wing, while very successful for flights near the speed of sound, is not a good shape for slow flying.

Because of the sweep, when the wing is at a high angle of attack (during the approach to land, for instance), there are very strong cross flows of air. The outer parts of the wing tend to stall before the inner wing. Such a tip stall can be disastrous, since the aircraft tends to roll over and may crash before the pilot can regain control. For this reason, aircraft with swept-back wings have many devices, such as wing leading and trailing edge flaps, slots, boundary layer fences and vortex generators, most of which are used only during take-off and landing (Figure 178).

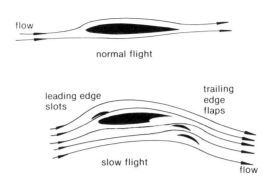

Sweptback wings tend to be difficult to control at low speeds, as when landing or taking off. Various kinds of flaps, slots and other devices are used to prevent flow separation.

178. Control of sweptback wings at low speed.

Some jet aircraft have used a delta-shaped wing. This shape has many advantages. The leading edge of the wing, which meets the air first, can be sharply swept back, but the triangular shape still produces good lift at very high angles of attack. In the chapter on kites, it was mentioned that a kite with very short span in relation to the chord (low aspect ratio), will fly quite well at an angle to the airflow of 40 degrees. This is the same for jet-powered aircraft at low speeds. The delta wing shape is also very strong and stiff, so it can be made very thin without losing strength. The thinner the wing, the better it is for very high-speed flight.

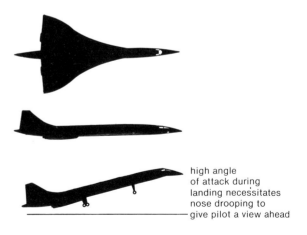

high angle of attack during landing necessitates nose drooping to give pilot a view ahead

179. The Concorde airliner, which has a 'delta' wing platform.

180 The Concorde taking off. Note the very high angle of attack of the delta wing, and the drooping nose which gives the pilot a good view ahead.

The Concorde is probably the best-known example of this type of wing (Figure 179 and Photo 180). When landing, the angle of attack is so high that the pilot's cockpit has to be tilted downwards to enable him to see the runway ahead. During the supersonic stages of the flight, the cockpit is raised and an additional shield slides over the windscreen, to keep the airflow smooth.

Another solution is to have a wing that can vary its angle of sweep (Figure 181). The F111 used by the RAAF is of this type. At near sonic and supersonic speeds, the wings are swept fully back. For slow flight, landing and take-off, the wings are moved to a nearly straight position and the danger of tip stalling is much less. Unfortunately all such devices are expensive and heavy, which tends to make them impractical for ordinary commercial aircraft.

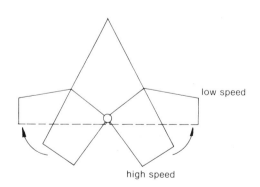

The angle of sweepback can be varied to give good control at low speeds and low drag at sonic or supersonic speeds.

181. The variable sweep wing.

182 The F-111 variable-sweep aircraft flown by the RAAF. In this photograph the wing is in the slow speed position, but the slanting lines visible near the roots of the wings show the angles of sweep that may be taken up at higher speeds. (RAAF)

The heat barrier

As described earlier, high speed missiles used in World War II became heated by their flight so that the metal of their skin became red hot. When shock waves form, the air is sharply compressed which causes very rapid heating. This heat passes to the aircraft surface, which is further heated by the friction of the flow. For aeroplanes flying faster than sound, heating of the skin is a very serious problem. Ordinary metals lose strength as they become hotter. The Concorde is close to the limits for normal aircraft materials. At Mach 2.0 the outer skin of the Concorde fuselage becomes hotter than 100°C. For flights at higher Mach numbers than this, different materials are required. Special alloys have been developed which will retain their strength and stiffness at high temperatures. These are used on some military aircraft. Above Mach 4, even stainless steels may not be adequate. Any crew and passengers, or cargo, must also be kept cool. Even if some kind of refrigeration system is installed, the heat drawn from the cabin has to be got rid of. One way of doing this is to use it to heat the fuel before pumping it into the motor. It is no good trying to cool the aircraft by means of ordinary radiators exposed to the air. The source of the heat is the friction caused by the high-speed flow of the air and the compression associated with the shock waves. To place a radiator in such a flow would cause even more heat to be generated, the radiator would then work in the opposite way to that intended, heating the interior of the cabin instead of cooling it.

Space craft returning to earth enter the atmosphere at very high velocities and the heating effect is very great. They have to be provided with heat shields which protect them. The space shuttle Columbia is skinned entirely with special ceramic material which can withstand great heat and at the same time insulate the metal underneath. Without this type of protection, re-entry would be impossible. Meteors which fall into the atmosphere from space burn up very rapidly and form so-called shooting stars. When air is heated to such temperatures, the molecules of the gases it contains, chiefly oxygen and nitrogen, break up and become ionised. This interrupts radio communication with space craft during the early phases of re-entry. The air resistance soon slows down the flight, and the final landing is made at subsonic speeds or, in the case of space capsules, even by parachute.

Things to do:

1   Break the sound barrier. There are many ways of setting off a small shock wave. Try clapping your hands, bursting a balloon or paper bag, cracking a whip (the tip moves at supersonic speed), fire a pop-gun etc. Think of other examples.

Things to find out:

1   Read about the Concorde airliner. Find out especially about the regulations governing its routes.
2   Find out who was the first pilot to fly faster than sound. What aircraft did he use?
3   Study the problems of re-entry to the atmosphere of space vehicles.

chapter 14

the future

To understand airflow is becoming more important. The old mysteries and superstitions have gone. People no longer imagine that there is anything magical about the winds or flying. Yet there are still mysteries. Much remains to be discovered about the way in which air flows. The weather itself is very largely a result of the flow of air over land and sea, hot and cold regions, and the general circulation of the atmosphere. The human race is still a very long way from understanding these large movements and even further from being able to control them.

On a smaller scale, much more attention needs to be given in future to designing buildings and other structures to withstand the wind. Cyclones and other storm winds can be predicted to some extent, but it should be possible for architects and engineers to build houses and office blocks which do not collapse when such winds arrive. To achieve this, research into the flow of air over structures must go on all the time. It is not enough to design each building separately as if the airflow near it was unaffected by other structures. As the Ferry-bridge disaster showed, several towers standing near to one another cause the flow to speed up in between to such an extent that the Bernoulli effect can greatly reduce the air pressure. The walls may be sucked out, or the wake of one tall building, with its wild and powerful vortices, may destroy another tower on the lee side. A whole town may be badly planned and exposed to damage and danger if the flow of the air around the groups of buildings is ignored.

Farmers already know a great deal about wind erosion, but still, on any windy day in the dry country of Australia and other similar regions of the Earth, great dust clouds form and these indicate the loss of vast quantities of irreplaceable soil. Ways of checking such losses are being improved all the time, but more needs to be done. Crops which can bind the soil together and hold it down are used; there may have to be more windbreaks of trees; perhaps hedges rather than wire fences will be needed in some areas to slow the wind down near the ground and save the soil.

moderate to high wind   high wind

Compare this map with a map of world population. Which regions seem most likely to develop wind power? Consider not only the available wind energy but also who will need the power.

183. A world map showing areas where much wind energy is available.

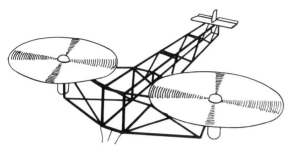

This type of kite may one day be flown to generate electricity from the high-level jetstream winds. The rotors would blow around like windmill sails, but, like an autogiro, would also lift the kite.

184. A gyro-kite design.

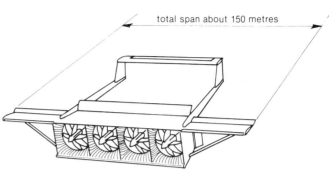

total span about 150 metres

A design by Dr C. Fletcher and Professor B. Roberts of Sydney University, for a very large power-generating kite, to fly in the jetstream above 10 km altitude. The windmill-like fans would be harnessed to generators and the electric current would be carried down to earth through the line.

185. Design for a power-generating kite.

As natural supplies of fuel oil begin to run out and become more and more costly, it is sure that one of the ways of supplying energy in the future will be to use the wind. There are already many small wind-driven electric generators of various designs. Some of them are not very efficient, but can be built easily and work well enough in regions far from other sources of power. More efficient windmill and wind turbine designs will be seen. The day may come when most of the electric power used in everyday life will come from wind-driven generators and solar-powered heaters.

Another way of saving costly fuel is to improve the airflow over land vehicles. Modern designs of motor cars are better than old ones, but are still very far from good, aerodynamically. Underneath the ordinary car, for instance, the airflow is very disturbed, and since people do not often consider this when buying a new car, little attention has been given to it by the stylists. Racing car designers have shown how the flow underneath can be used both to increase the car's top speed and also to make it safer. The Bernoulli effect can be used to keep the car more firmly on the road, instead of lifting it off at high speed. More heavy goods vehicles will be fitted with drag-saving devices, and some re-designing of the shape of heavy trucks will probably save even more fuel. It may turn out, in the long run, that railway trains, travelling at high speeds on very good tracks, will use fuel more economically than road vehicles, simply because a long line of squarish cars one behind the other causes less air resistance than a similar number of separate trucks on the road.

On the sea, it is very likely that sailing ships will return, or at least that many cargo ships will carry sails and use them to save fuel when the winds are favourable. It has already been proved possible for a ship with modern sails, designed like aeroplane wings, to cut its use of fuel. By using weather reports from satellites and following the pressure pattern shown on the weather map, the old problem of being becalmed for days has been much reduced. This kind of navigation may become the general rule. Ships will still be provided with engines for the occasions when the wind does fail and for use in narrow waters among other shipping, but sailors may once again come to rely chiefly on the wind.

Sailing and board sailing, for sport, will continue and very probably as the cost of fuel for motor boats and motor yachts increases, the small sailing vessel will become even more popular. The same may be true in the air. Power flying for pleasure is already becoming much more expensive. Hang gliding and sailplane soaring are cheaper and more economical. Studies of airflow connected with improved sailplanes have shown many ways of saving drag. Using these discoveries, powered flight is now possible with small motors using very little fuel. Some modern light aeroplanes, with wings like those of a sailplane, can fly just as fast and as high as older types with rather short wings, of low aspect ratio, bulky fuselages and powerful motors. Before long it may be quite usual for a sporting aeroplane to turn off its motor, when there are useable thermals, and continue by soaring. At the same time, sailplane pilots may get used to the idea of carrying a small motor to take off and to save them from landing far away from base when they find the upcurrents dying unexpectedly. This will save fuel in the long run since no powerful aeroplane will be needed for launching and after a landing away, no long towed journey, by air or road, will be needed to get the sailplane home. Parachuting and skydiving will also continue. As parachutes become more efficient and controllable, they may be used for soaring flights like hang gliders. Getting the skydiver up to a height from which to jump will remain rather costly. Perhaps balloons and airships will be more often used for this.

In commercial aviation, there are still many ways in which the airliner can be made more efficient. Some engineers believe that future transport aircraft will be much cheaper to operate, in terms of fuel use, than those which are common now. The future passenger aircraft will have new wing sections and there may be winglets at the tips to reduce the vortices and save drag. Probably the new wings and fuselages will be made very smooth and may be polished and cleaned before each flight. When a wing is viewed from directly above, or a plan of the wing is drawn from this angle, the resulting shape is termed the *planform*. The planform is found to have important effects on drag, especially at supersonic speeds. New types of planform will be developed, and new ways of controlling airliners with sweptback wings during the slow phases of their flight.

It is not at all sure that there will be more supersonic airliners like the Concorde. This famous aircraft has proved, so far, very costly to operate and the unpleasant 'sonic boom' caused by the shock waves it produces has prevented its flying over many countries. Still, some aeronautical experts believe that future airliners will be built which can fly at even higher Mach numbers and use less fuel. They may have extreme forms of delta wing shape, or perhaps the wings will be swept forward; they would have the advantage of working safely at low speeds as well as producing low drag at Mach 2 or 3.

Another interesting possibility is the return of the lighter-than-air ship, in a new form which takes more account of aerodynamic principles. The old *airships* of the period 1900 to 1937 were designed to get all their lift from a light gas such as hydrogen or helium. Otherwise their hulls were made to

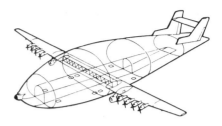

Lift would come from the light gas in the very large body, but the forward drive provided by the turboprop and turbojet engines would generate aerodynamic lift over the body and wing also. Flight speed would be slow but very large cargoes could be carried. It is even possible that small aeroplanes could be used to ferry passengers to and from the mother ship, which would rarely need to land.

186. A suggested design for an airship combined with a wing. (W.J. White, *Airships for the Future*, Sterling Publishing, New York, 1979.)

slip smoothly through the air with as little drag as possible. Sometimes, by trimming the huge hull to a positive angle of attack, some aerodynamic lift could be obtained, which was useful but not often necessary. Development of airships ended suddenly in 1937 when the German liner, 'Hindenburg', which had made many successful passenger flights across the Atlantic from Germany to America, burst into flames and crashed with much loss of life. Hydrogen, a flammable gas, was used to provide the lift. Helium, which will not burn, would be much safer. The airship of the future may be something like that shown in Figure 186. The hull itself will be given a flattish shape, so that it will act to some extent like a low aspect ratio wing. In addition, long wings of higher aspect ratio, carrying the engines, will extend out sideways. Such a monstrous ship, combining the lift of the gas in its hull with the aerodynamic lift, should be capable of carrying very large loads, perhaps even as much as a modern seagoing cargo ship. Although slow in flight, it would complete its air journeys from continent to continent in a day or so and would be capable of delivering its cargoes at any place on the land. A ship of this size might act as an aerial base for smaller aircraft which could ferry passengers and goods to and from any place below. The large craft itself might rarely need to land. Another possible airship of the future could have a delta planform. This too would get most of its lift from its gas, but the wing-shaped form would provide much additional lifting ability.

In outer space there is no atmosphere or airflow, yet the Columbia space shuttle was designed as a rocket-powered glider. After its flight in orbit round the earth, it descends into the air, under control like a glider or an aeroplane with its engine off, and lands on a prepared airfield or smooth salt lake bed. It is very likely that such gliding flights from space will become quite frequent. One of the most modern of all flying machines thus employs the same principles of airflow as those that drive a windmill or a sailing boat, and which George Cayley realised, more than 150 years ago, would enable a glider to fly. If mankind ever does reach other planets with breathable atmospheres, no doubt the same principles will be found to operate there too.

Things to do:

1 With friends, discuss what it may be like to live in the future, if all aerodynamic knowledge is used to the full. It may be a good idea to organise small groups to study various special aspects of the matter in detail. Consider not only how aerodynamics may be used to make transport more efficient at sea, on land and in the air, but look also at building design, inside and out, and all kinds of sport where airflow and air resistance has to be met. At the end of the special study group periods, the outcome might be a plan for an imaginary city or state of the future. This could be a paper plan with drawings and explanatory text, or it may be worth building a model to show all the features of life in such an 'air-conscious' world.

glossary / index

The italicised numbers refer to illustrations. The other references are to page numbers, where the catchword in question has been italicised in the text. Words printed in bold type in the text of the glossary are index entries in their own right.

Aerofoil 64
An aerofoil (sometimes airfoil) is any surface shaped in such a way that it extends into an airflow so as to generate some useful force. Hence a wing on an aeroplane is an aerofoil, but so are the wing-like shapes used on some racing cars to increase road holding. Often the word aerofoil is used to stand for aerofoil section which is the shape of the wing in cross section. See also **wing profile**.

Ailerons 68
The hinged control surfaces mounted on the trailing edges of the wings of an aeroplane or glider, near the tips. As the aileron on one side hinges up, the one on the other wing hinges down. This banks the aircraft and causes it to turn. The ailerons are controlled by means of the pilot's control column or joystick. A rightward movement of the stick causes the right aileron to hinge up. The right wing then goes down, to turn to the right.

Airship 108
An aircraft which gains its support from a light gas such as hydrogen, helium or hot air. Engines drive the ship along and the shape of the hull is such that it creates little drag. Some new designs for airships, not yet actually built, gain some lift from the gas and some also from aerofoils or even from the hull itself, trimmed to a positive angle of attack.

Altitude 12
Altitude is the term used in aviation for height above the ground or, more often, height above mean sea level as measured when the altimeter in the aircraft is set to the International Standard Atmosphere figure of 1013.2 millibars.

Anemometer 6
An instrument used for measuring the speed of the wind.

Angle of attack 31
The angle at which any aerofoil (wing, sail, etc) is inclined to the flow of the air. If the angle is too small, little useful force will be generated. If the angle of attack is too large the flow will separate and the result will be a stall.

Aspect ratio 33
The ratio of the total span of an aerofoil (wing, sail etc) to the mean chord. A convenient formula for working out this ratio is to divide the square of the span by the total area. Hence:

$$A = \frac{span^2}{area}$$

A wing with large span and narrow chord is thus a high-aspect-ratio wing.

Atmosphere 10
The sphere of air which encloses the earth.

Autogiro 86
A type of aircraft which gains its support from a free-spinning rotor. The autogiro is driven forwards through the air by an engine with an ordinary propeller. The rotor spins like a windmill rotor and lifts the craft. See also **gyrocopter**.

Barometer 15
An instrument for measuring air pressure, usually in millibars.

Bearing off *53*
In sailing, when a ship turns away from the wind, it is said to bear off, the opposite of **luffing up**.

Beating against the wind 31
No sailing ship can sail directly into the wind but it is possible to make headway at an angle to the wind by beating. Some types of sailing vessel are better at this than others

and can sail close to the wind. To navigate in the desired direction against the wind it is necessary to **tack**, which involves **going about** at the end of a beat and beating on the other tack, in zig-zag fashion.

Bernoulli's theorem 7
Daniel Bernoulli discovered the relation between speed of flow and pressure in a fluid, such as air. The faster the flow speed, the less the pressure. This is expressed in the equation:

$$p + \frac{\varrho}{2} V^2 = \text{constant}$$

In the equation, p stands for pressure, V for flow velocity and ϱ for the fluid density.

Biplane 78
A type of aeroplane or glider with two sets of wings arranged one above the other. This enables a large wing area to be used with a very light and stiff structure. Struts and wire bracing are used to make the framework rigid. Unfortunately the struts and wires create much drag, and the wings tend to interfere with one another so the monoplane is much more efficient for high-speed flight.

Centre of pressure 30
Also called centre of effort this is a point on a sail or wing at which all the forces may be taken as acting. Although in fact the aerodynamic loads on the surface are spread over the whole of it, it is often convenient to think of them all as concentrated at the centre of pressure, since this helps in understanding the forces involved in trimming and controlling the craft.

Chord 33
The dimension of a wing or any other wing-like surface, measured in a direction parallel to the direction of movement.

Cirrus clouds 10
Very high, feathery or streaky clouds which are actually formed by innumerable tiny ice particles carried along by the high-speed winds which often blow at such heights.

Compressor 93
An engine used to force air under pressure into a smaller volume, so increasing its density. Compressors are often simply air pumps, but those used in **turbojet** engines are usually of the rotary vane type.

Cumulus clouds 10
Any heaped-up form of cloud, commonly with a fairly dark, flattish base. Such clouds are formed by rising air currents, especially **thermals**. They usually grow for some time and then begin to evaporate and disappear. In some conditions they may grow very large to become cumulo-nimbus thunderstorm clouds.

Cyclic pitch control 88
The means by which helicopter rotor blades are made to change their angles of attack to the airflow as they rotate. This equalises the lift force on each side as the helicopter moves forward. Without some such control, single rotor helicopters would be incapable of controlled flight.

Cyclone 2
A very large, severe circular storm associated with a very deep low-pressure region in the atmosphere. The cyclone is a very large vortex or whirlwind, which brings very severe winds and causes great destruction. In South-east Asia north of the equator, cyclones are called typhoons, and in other regions they are termed hurricanes. All these terms refer to the same type of huge, destructive, circular storm.

Darrius rotor 79
A type of wind-driven turbine, consisting of flexible aerofoils mounted on a vertical axis so that the rotor spins in any wind direction. In some conditions such rotors are more efficient than the simpler **S rotor**.

Density 11
The mass of a substance in relation to the volume of space it occupies, is its density. Most solid and liquid substances change their density very little under normal conditions, but gases, such as air, are very variable in density and change with variations of pressure and temperature.

Dihedral 52
When viewed from directly in front, most aeroplanes and gliders, and some kites, have the wings set at a slight tilt so that the outer tips are higher than the roots. This is the dihedral, and it is used to give the aircraft some lateral, or sideways rocking, stability.

Drag 18, 50
The resistance of the air to anything moving

through it is termed drag. It is usually regarded as the great enemy of aerodynamic engineers, but can be useful when aircraft or cars need extra braking effect, which can be achieved by extending airbrakes.

Downwash 53
As a wing passes through the air, giving lift, it deflects the flow downwards. The downward turning extends in all directions both behind and ahead of the wing. This is the downwash effect.

Elevator 67
The hinged control surface usually mounted on the horizontal tail surface of an aeroplane or glider, and used to control the angle of attack of the main wing. The elevator is connected to the pilot's control column, so a forward movement of the column lowers the elevator, raises the tail and so reduces the angle of attack of the wing. This normally causes the aircraft to gain speed. Sometimes the elevator may be mounted ahead of the mainplane, as on the original Wright brothers' aeroplanes.

Equilibrium 51
A condition in which all the forces acting on any object are balanced so that there is no change in the speed or direction of movement.

Fantail 39
A small windmill rotor mounted at right angles to the main rotor and geared in such a way that if the wind changes, the fantail turns and moves the main turbine to face the new direction.

Flaps 68
Hinged surfaces mounted along the trailing, or sometimes the leading, edges of an aircraft wing. Unlike **ailerons**, the flaps on each side always move up or down together. They are used to adjust the camber or curvature of the wing to suit different speeds of flight. In landing, they are usually lowered fully to create more drag and delay the stall, permitting a slow touch-down speed.

Flutter 6
Unless carefully balanced and stiff, any control surface or even the entire wing or tail of an aeroplane or glider may begin to flutter to and fro in a manner similar to a flag fluttering in a stiff breeze. Structures such as bridges may also flutter in strong winds. The result is usually disastrous but the causes are now well known and trouble can be avoided.

Fuselage 67
The body of an aeroplane or glider, usually housing the crew, cargo and passengers.

Glider chapter 9
Any free-flying, heavier-than-air craft which flies without an engine is a glider. The term thus includes both **hang gliders** and **sailplanes**, but not **kites**.

Glide ratio 62
The relationship of the distance covered through the air to the height lost, either by a glider or by a powered aeroplane with its engine throttled back; usually expressed as a ratio, such as 10:1 or 36:1. The higher the figure, the more efficient the gliding performance.

Going about 31
Turning a sailing vessel onto another tack.

Gyrocopter 87
A small **autogiro**.

Hang glider *121*
A simple glider from which the pilot hangs in a harness.

Helicopter *152, 153*
An aircraft which gains both its lift and its thrust from large power-driven rotors, unlike the **autogiro** which relies on a free-spinning, unpowered rotor. Helicopters with only a single lifting rotor normally require a tail rotor to counteract the **torque reaction**.

Kinetic energy 3
The energy possessed by any moving mass as a result of its motion.

Kite chapter 7
An aircraft which flies tethered by a line.

Leeway 29
A sailing ship or boat heading in any direction other than directly downwind is pushed sideways off its course to some extent by the wind. The amount of this sideways movement is the leeway. Vessels with long, narrow hulls and deep keels usually make less leeway than short-hulled, shallow-draft vessels.

Lenticular clouds 66
Large, whalebacked clouds aligned across the wind, formed by atmospheric **waves** in the lee of ranges of hills or mountains.

Lift 50
Normally, the force created by a wing or rotor on an aircraft, and directed more or less upwards. However, when the aircraft is in an unusual position, the actual direction of the force may be sideways or even downwards, but is still termed lift by the engineer.

Luffing up *54*
When a sailing vessel turns its head towards the wind, it is said to be luffing up.

Mach number 98
Named after Ernst Mach (1838–1916), the Mach number relates the velocity of an object moving through a fluid to the speed of sound in the fluid. A Mach number of 1.0 indicates the speed of sound, 0.5 represents half the speed of sound, 2.0 twice sonic speed, and so on.

Manometer 6
A simple device for comparing the pressure at two different points. Normally one end of a simple U-shaped tube containing liquid is left open to the local atmosphere and the other end of the U-tube is connected to the point where the pressure is to be compared. The liquid in the tube moves up or down on one side or the other depending on the pressure difference.

Pitch 38, 80
This term has two distinct uses in aeronautics.
It may refer to the angle of a propeller blade or windmill vane to the plane of rotation. A fine pitch indicates the blade is at a small angle to this plane; a coarse pitch indicates a large angle.
The other use of the term refers to the nose-up or nose-down movement of an aircraft, controlled by the **elevator**.

Planform 53, 108
When a wing or vehicle is viewed from directly above or below, or drawn as if seen from such a position, the resulting shape is its planform.

Potential energy 3
The energy of a mass due to its position.

Precession *83*
Any spinning object, such as a wheel or propeller or boomerang, resists any attempt to change the direction of its axis of rotation. A force twisting the axis one way produces a strong reaction tending to turn the axis at 90 degrees to the direction of the force. This accounts for the circular flight path of boomerangs and also can cause problems of control for aeroplanes with large propellers or rotary engines of the type used in the early days of aviation.

Pulse jet engine 93
A simple form of jet reaction motor which gives thrust in a rapid series of sharp pulses. Only very simple flap valves are needed at the air intake. Such motors are very noisy and wasteful of fuel.

Pusher propeller 80
A propeller on an aeroplane which pushes the aircraft along, in a manner similar to a normal boat propeller.

Ramjet engine 101
A very simple type of jet reaction motor which has no moving parts. The air is compressed by the rapid movement of the intake itself, and fuel is burned to create the jet. Such a motor will work only if it is accelerated to high velocities before being started.

Reaching 31, 32
Sailing across the wind direction. This is normally the fastest point of sailing.

Reaction thrust 92
The thrust created by the rapid ejection of a large mass of air or gas through the tail pipe of a jet engine or rocket motor.

Red line speed 78
See VNE.

Relative flow 38
When a ship, car, aeroplane, or any other object moves through the air, the airflow (wind) felt by those on board is different in both strength and direction from the true wind measured on land at a stationary site. The flow over the moving object is the relative wind.

Resolution of forces 29
Any single force may be regarded as the pro-

duct of two forces acting at right angles to one another, the supposed pair of forces having the same effect as the single force. To find the strengths and directions of the resolved forces it is necessary to construct a diagram with the original single force represented by the diagonal of a rectangle in which the resolved components will be represented by the sides of the rectangle.

Running before the wind   28
A sailing vessel which is sailing with the wind behind it is running before the wind. The speed of travel is limited by the speed of the wind itself.

Sailplane   63
A very efficient glider, capable of soaring and used for long-distance and high-altitude flights, and for racing in competitions.

S rotor   37
A type of wind-driven turbine, invented by S.J. Savonius in 1921.

Separated flow   2
Flow of any fluid which breaks away from the surface of the object it is flowing over and becomes very turbulent, is termed separated flow. (See also **stalling**)

Shock wave   40, 100
The compression wave caused by any movement through air at sonic or supersonic speed.

Slope soaring   65
Soaring by a glider or sailplane over the windward face of a hill or mountain range, where an upcurrent is created by the wind rising to pass over the hill.

Soaring   65
Gaining altitude in a glider or sailplane by using upcurrents of air. (See also **slope soaring, thermal, wave soaring**.)

Sonic bang   101
The loud bang (also called sonic boom) heard when a supersonic aircraft or missile travelling at supersonic speed passes by.

Span   63
The dimension of a pair of wings or any winglike surface from the extreme tip of one wing to the other tip, at right angles to the direction of movement.

Spinnaker   29
The very large, roughly triangular sail used by yachts when running before the wind, which is useless when reaching or beating against the wind.

Square Law   7, 19
The effects of fluid flow (at speeds well below that of sound) are proportional to the square of the velocity. Hence as the speed of flow rises, the aerodynamic reaction increases very rapidly.

Stalling   31
When the airflow over a wing or sail separates and becomes turbulent, the wing or sail is stalled.

Standard atmosphere   14
A table of figures representing an artificial atmosphere, used in aeronautics for design purposes and for the setting of instruments in aircraft for air traffic control.

Stratosphere   14
The layer of the atmosphere immediately above the troposphere, in which the temperature remains almost constant with height at about $-57.3°C$.

Streamlined flow   2
Air (or any fluid) flowing smoothly without violent turbulence or sharp changes of direction.

Tacking   31
Making progress in a sailing vessel against the wind by following a zig-zag course, beating first one way, then going about and beating on the other tack.

Temperature inversion   14
A common condition in the lowest levels of the atmosphere, when the ground has cooled overnight. The air near the ground is cooler than that some distance above, whereas in general the temperature at high levels is less than that lower down. Slight temperature inversions are usual on most mornings but 'break' during the day as the ground warms up. A severe temperature inversion may persist all day and is often associated with fog and serious air pollution problems at ground level.

Terminal velocity   77
The maximum possible speed attainable by

an aeroplane or glider in a prolonged vertical dive.

Thermal 66
An upward current of air caused by the heating of the ground by the sun, so warming the air and causing it to rise. Thermals are much used by sailplanes for soaring.

Thrust 51
The force produced by a propeller or jet reaction motor, which drives an aircraft forwards.

Tornado 2
A fierce, very strong and dangerous but small whirlwind, often arising during a thunderstorm and capable of doing great damage over a relatively small area.

Torque 82
The force which turns a propeller, rotor, or the driving wheels of a road vehicle.

Torque reaction *146*
Associated with any force is a reaction, which in the case of torque appears as a force tending to rotate the vehicle being driven. Thus a helicopter requires a tail rotor to counteract the torque reaction of its main rotor. A propeller driven clockwise will tend to produce an anti-clockwise reaction tending to roll the aircraft over. The torque reaction from the driving wheels of a car tends to pitch the car 'nose up'.

Tractor propeller 80
An aircraft propeller which pulls the aircraft forward.

Triplane 78
An aeroplane or glider with three pairs of wings, one above the other. (See also **biplane**.)

Troposphere 14
The lowest layer of the atmosphere in which, except for local temperature inversions, the air becomes cooler with height.

Turbine 38
Any rotating machine driven by a fluid flow is a turbine.

Turbojet engine 93
A jet reaction engine consisting essentially of a turbine driving a compressor, so that air drawn in through the intake and compressed by the compressor is then heated by burning fuel in the combustion chamber to expand and form the jet which drives the turbine and creates thrust.

Turboprop engine 94
A turbojet engine in which most of the power of the jet is absorbed by an enlarged turbine, which then drives both the compressor and a propeller to provide thrust.

VNE 78
In aviation, the velocity which is never to be exceeded during the operation of an aircraft. Flight at higher speeds, while often possible, is likely to damage the aircraft.

Vortices 3, 18
Singular — vortex: a roughly circular whirling of fluid, often occurring on a small scale in regions of **separated flow**. However, all forms of rotary flow, including **tornadoes, cyclones** and the flow of air round atmospheric low pressure areas, are also vortices.

Wave 66
A wave (lee wave, standing wave) in the atmosphere often forms in the lee of a range of hills or mountains. Such waves are frequently marked by **lenticular clouds**.

Wave soaring 66
The use of lee waves by sailplanes to gain altitude.

Wing profile 64
Also called wing section or aerofoil section, this is the cross-sectional form of a wing.